Rigorous Schools and Classrooms
Leading the Way

Ronald Williamson
Barbara R. Blackburn

Routledge
Taylor & Francis Group
New York London

First published 2010 by Eye On Education

Published 2013 by Routledge
711 Third Avenue, New York, NY 10017, USA
2 Park Square, Milton Park, Abingdon, Oxon OX14 4RN

Routledge is an imprint of the Taylor & Francis Group, an informa business

Library of Congress Cataloging-in-Publication Data

Williamson, Ronald D.
   Rigorous schools and classrooms : leading the way / Ronald Williamson and Barbara R. Blackburn.
      p.   cm.
   ISBN 978-1-59667-145-4
   1. School improvement programs—United States. 2. Educational leadership—United States. I. Blackburn, Barbara R., 1961– II. Title.
   LB2822.82.W56 2010
   371.2'07—dc22   2009050787

ISBN: 978-1-596-67145-4 (pbk)

Dedication

Ron dedicates this book to his wife, Marsha,
whose encouragement, support and understanding
make our life together so special.

Barbara lovingly dedicates this book to her husband, Pete,
who brings joy to every moment of her life. His modeling
of servant leadership in each aspect of his life inspires me.

Together, we dedicate this book to the courageous
principals and teachers who are making a difference
in the lives of their students every day of the week.

Meet the Authors

Ronald Williamson is the author of more than 100 articles, chapters, papers and books. A professor of leadership and counseling at Eastern Michigan University, Ron works with schools throughout the country on school improvement projects. He previously taught at the University of North Carolina at Greensboro and was a teacher, principal, and executive director of instruction in the Ann Arbor, Michigan public schools.

Ron also served as executive director of the National Middle School Association, as a member of Middle Level Council of the National Association of Secondary School Principals, and as president of the National Forum to Accelerate Middle grades Reform. He received the Gruhn-Long-Melton Award from NASSP in recognition of lifetime achievement in secondary school leadership. If you'd like information about Ron and his work contact him through his website: www.ronwilliamson.com.

Barbara R. Blackburn is the author of seven best-selling books, including *Rigor is Not a Four-Letter Word, Classroom Motivation from A to Z, Classroom Instruction from A to Z*, and *Literacy from A to Z*. She has taught elementary, middle, and high school students and has served as an educational consultant for three publishing companies. She is now on the faculty at the University of North Carolina at Charlotte, where she teaches graduate classes and collaborates with area schools. She also regularly presents keynote addresses and workshops for teachers and administrators. Her workshops are lively and engaging and filled with practical information. For more information and resources, contact Barbara at www.barbarablackburnonline.com.

Together, Ron and Barbara are the authors of the best-selling book *The Principalship from A to Z* and a regular monthly column, *Everyday Leadership* for *Principal Leadership*. They work together to conduct rigor audits and help schools develop plans for improving rigor. Tools and information regarding rigor audits are available at www.rigorineducation.com.

Acknowledgments

We'd like to thank the following people who encouraged us and supported our work:

- Our families and friends for their encouragement. We could never have finished without your support and your willingness to listen as we turned our ideas into a manuscript.
- Bob Sickles for his confidence and gentle reminders about the book.
- Colleagues in the Department of Leadership and Counseling at Eastern Michigan University and in the Department of Middle, Secondary, and K-12 Education at the University of North Carolina at Charlotte. You are a continued source of support and positive reinforcement.
- The thoughtful reviewers who read early drafts and provided us and offered helpful suggestions: Amanda Heinemann , Valerie Henning-Piedmonte, Brenda Shelton, Laura Springer.
- Robert Blackburn for his expertise and support when we developed Chapter 9 on advocacy.
- Dave Strauss who created the compass graphic for the cover.
- National Association of Secondary School Principals for the opportunity to write a monthly column in *Principal Leadership* where we shared some of our strategies for increasing rigor in schools.
- The leaders in Area 10 of the Chicago Public Schools for their insightful feedback.
- The principals and teachers throughout the country who talked with us about their schools and their efforts to improve rigor. We value your work and appreciate the specific strategies you shared. Your ideas made this book more practical and useful to people like you.

Table of Contents

Introduction xi

1 Leadership for Rigor: More Than a Mandate. 1
  The Many Roles of a School Leader 1
    Instructional Leader 2
    Human Resource Developer 2
    Change Agent 3
  Change as a Journey, Not an Event 3
  The BASE Planning Model 3
  The COMPASS Model 4
    C—Creating a Positive and Supportive Culture 4
    O—Ownership and Shared Vision. 5
    M—Managing Data 5
    P—Professional Development 6
    A—Advocacy. 7
    S—Shared Accountability 7
    S—Structures 8
  Getting Started 9
    Check Your Own Assumptions. 9
    Use Positive and Supportive Leadership Behaviors 10
  Final Thoughts 11

2 A Rationale for Rigor 13
  Myths About Rigor. 14
    Myth #1: Lots of Homework Is a Sign of Rigor 14
    Myth #2: Rigor Means Doing More 15
    Myth #3: Rigor is Not for Everyone 15
    Myth #4: Providing Support Means Lessening Rigor 16
  The Call for Rigor. 16
  More Recent Discussion of Rigor 18
  Beginning the Work on an Agenda of Rigor. 21
    What Does It Mean? 22
    How to Get There? 23
      Courses and Course Content. 23
      Assessments 25
      Teacher/Student Interaction and Support. 25
      Related Issues. 26
    Where Do I Go From Here? 27

3 Recognizing Rigor...29
    Expecting Students to Learn at High Levels 34
        Challenging Curriculum 34
        High Levels of Instruction.................................35
        Adult Behaviors 37
    Supporting Students to Learn at High Levels 38
        Scaffolding Within Lessons 39
        Incorporating Motivational Elements 39
        Addressing Strategic Knowledge...........................40
        Providing Extra Help 40
    Ensuring Students Demonstrate Learning at High Levels..........41
        Increased Student Engagement 41
        Clear Standards and Rubrics..............................42
        Challenging Assessments 43
        Multiple Options to Demonstrate Understanding..............43
    Final Thoughts 44

4 The BASE Planning Model 45
    Step 1: Beginning the Planning..................................46
        Use an Inclusive Process 47
        Be Clear About Group Operations..........................47
        Identify a Process for Making Decisions 48
        Provide a Common Base of Information.....................48
        Anchor Your Plan in a Shared Vision.......................48
        Commit to the Use of Data 49
    Step 2: Act to Implement the Plan 50
        Have a Plan for Monitoring the Implementation................51
        Nurture a Collegial Culture................................53
        Remove Barriers to Action.................................55
        Constructively Deal with Conflict 55
        Establish Accountability for Results.........................56
    Step 3: Sustain Success..57
        Continue to Provide Support for Success 58
        Create a Culture of Continuous Improvement.................59
        Use Data to Study the Results.............................59
        Identify Successes and Celebrate 60
        Other Ways to Sustain Success 61
    Step 4: Evaluate and Adjust 61
        Ensure Positive Dynamics Among School Personnel 62
        Data, Data, Data 63
        Share What You Are Doing 64
    Final Thoughts 65

5 Culture...67
  What does a rigorous culture look like? 68
  What is the role of the leader? 70
  What are the symbolic aspects of a rigorous culture?..............70
    Rituals and Ceremonies..72
    Heroes and Heroines 73
    Stories and Tales 74
    Reward System 75
      Summary of Symbolic Elements..............................76
  What are the structures that support a rigorous culture?..........77
  Final Thoughts 80

6 Ownership and Shared Vision 81
  Benefits of Cultivating Ownership 82
    Determining Involvement.......................................84
    Forming the Team and Getting Started 84
    Reduce Isolation and Build Collaborative Relationships 85
    Developing a Shared Vision of a Rigorous School...............85
      A Personal Vision of Rigor................................86
      Vision Letters 86
    Thinking About a Shared Vision................................87
    Creating or Recommitting to a School-Wide Vision 88
    Seeking Agreement About Decision on Rigor 89
  Final Thoughts 91

7 Managing Data...93
  Step 1: Determine What You Want to Know..........................94
  Step 2: Decide How You Will Collect Data 96
    Ways to Collect Data..97
      Data Collection Tools 98
      Collect Your Data..105
  Step 3: Analyze the Data/Results................................106
    Force Field Analysis 107
  Step 4: Set Priorities and Goals................................109
  Final Thoughts 110

8 Professional Development...111
  Contemporary Professional Development 111
  Key Lessons from Award-Winning Schools 112
  How do these elements support
  your efforts toward increased rigor?............................112
  Professional Learning Communities 114

Step One: Align Expectations with High Standards 118
Step Two: Develop Consistent Expectations 121
PRESS Forward Model for Action Planning. 122
Final Thoughts 124

9 **Advocacy** **125**
Why Be an Advocate? 125
First Steps. 126
Designing an Advocacy Plan 127
Stakeholders 128
Internal Stakeholders 129
External Stakeholders. 129
Movers and Shakers. 131
Build a Network 132
Advocacy Tools. 134
The One-Page Fact Sheet 134
Elevator Talk 136
Advocacy with Parents and Families 137
Talking with Your School Board. 140
Advocacy and the Media. 140
Advocacy and Emerging Technology 141
Advocacy Scorecard. 142
Final Thoughts 143

10 **Shared Accountability** **145**
Supporting Teachers and Other Staff. 146
Overcoming Resistance 146
Have a Clear, Concrete Result 149
Building Accountability into Everyday Routines 149
Accountability Through Supervisory Practices 150
Accountability Through Professional Development. 153
Accountability Through School Improvement. 153
Accountability Through Work with Families and Community. . . 154
Accountability for Students. 157
Focus and Refocus the Conversation. 158
It Starts and Ends with Me 159
Final Thoughts 160

11 **Structures to Support Rigor**. **161**
Professional Learning Communities 161
Time for Collaboration. 162
Organizing to Provide Collaborative Time. 164
Elementary School Examples 164
Scheduling Special Classes 164

      Parallel Schedule 164
   Secondary School Examples 165
      School-Within-A-School 165
      Organization of Curricular Departments 166
      Common Planning for Content Teachers. 166
Your School's Schedule as a Tool to Increase Rigor 166
Schedules that Support a Rigorous School 167
   Block Schedules. 168
   Alternating Day Schedules 169
   Trimester Schedules 170
Structures for Extra Support. 171
   Example 1: Student Rewards Program 171
   Example 2: Student Recognition Program 171
   Example 3: Academic Success Time. 172
Motivating Unmotivated Students 172
Getting Extra Help and Support 173
Structures to Support Families 175
Structures to Support the Leader 175
Final Thoughts 176

12 Challenges and Opportunities **177**
Resistance from Stakeholders 178
   Understand the Resistance 179
   Check Your Own Commitment. 180
   Work to Change Attitudes 181
      What a Leader Can Do 182
   Focus the Conversation on Students 183
Grading 183
Stable or Declining Resources. 186
Turnover in Leadership 187
   Expand Your Definition of Leadership 187
   Develop Leadership Capacity. 188
   Commit and Recommit to the Vision. 189
Final Thoughts 189

References. **191**

Free Downloads

Many of the tools discussed and displayed in this book are also available on the Routledge website as Adobe Acrobat files. Permission has been granted to purchasers of this book to download these tools and print them.

You can access these downloads by visiting www.routledge.com/9781596671454 and click on the Free Downloads tab.

List of Free Downloads

Rubric for Gauging Progress Toward Rigor. 30
Comparing Standards and Expectations 35
Recognizing Rigor Certificate. 76
Crosswalk of Data Collection. 105
Action Plan Template for Use of Data. 109
Evaluating and Adjusting the Curriculum. 120
PRESS Forward Template 123
Advocacy Scorecard. 142
Classroom Observation Form 150
Leadership Self-Assessment. 179

Introduction

Rigorous Schools and Classrooms: Leading the Way is a companion to Barbara's *Rigor is Not a Four-Letter Word*. In that book, Barbara described a wide range of instructional strategies that can be used to increase rigor at the classroom level. She used five categories of recommendations, and provided five specific strategies within each category, so that teachers could immediately increase rigor in their classroom, no matter what grade level or subject they teach.

Categories of Classroom-Based Recommendations

♦ Raise Level of Content
♦ Increase Complexity
♦ Give Support and Scaffolding
♦ Open Your Focus
♦ Raise Expectations

From: Blackburn, 2008

However, as we work with schools, we are constantly asked, "How do we move beyond the individual classroom to increase rigor in our school or district?" This book is our response to that question. Our focus in this book is straightforward: to provide school leaders and teachers with a practical guide that you can use to work together to make your school more rigorous. Just as *Rigor is NOT a Four-Letter Word* is filled with immediately applicable, classroom-based strategies, this book is filled with immediately applicable, school-based strategies.

The organization is simple. Chapter One: Leadership is More than a Mandate includes a brief description of key leadership skills, the BASE model of change, and the COMPASS tools for increasing rigor. We finish with suggestions for navigating the journey you will face as a leader committed to increasing rigor in your school or district. At times, you will see us use the term leader, at other times we will use principal. We have developed the book for principals and all other education leaders: assistant principals, curriculum specialists, superintendents, instructional coaches, teacher-leaders, etc. We hope you will find that our broader focus only increases the usability of the book.

The chapters are organized in a consistent way. You begin with a short introduction, are then introduced to several tools that you can use and finally, you have an opportunity to learn from other school leaders in a section called "Leadership in Action."

We believe strongly in providing every student with access to a rigorous educational experience and know that courageous principals, leaders and skillful teachers are the key to making that a reality. We hope you find these strategies helpful as you work together to improve the rigor in your school.

1

Leadership for Rigor:
More Than a Mandate

Whether you are a principal, assistant principal, curriculum coordinator, or some other type of school leader, you likely have times that you feel caught between multiple roles. Although your most visible role may be as a manager, in charge of the day-to-day operations of the school, the more important role is your role as instructional leader. As we begin our discussion of leading rigor, we will discuss this multi-faceted role and provide several planning tools that you can use to work with your teachers and families to improve rigor. We will also introduce our BASE and COMPASS models that you can use to positively impact the rigor of your school.

The Many Roles of a School Leader

It is clear that the principal can significantly impact his/her school (Davis, Darling-Hammond, LaPointe, and Meyerson, 2005; Leithwood, Louis, Anderson and Wahlstrom, 2004), the instructional program and the culture and climate. Your impact is less direct on student learning but through your work with teachers, families, and other stakeholders, you are able to transform your school into a vibrant, engaging learning environment.

In *The Principalship from A to Z* (Williamson & Blackburn, 2009), we suggested that three of the most important roles are instructional leader, human resource developer, and change agent. Each of these roles is critical when leading the way to a more rigorous learning environment.

Roles of School Leaders

♦ Instructional Leader
♦ Human Resource Developer
♦ Change Agent

Instructional Leader

Improving instruction is one of the most essential ways to increase rigor in your school. We've found that leaders who hold high expectations for student learning, visit classrooms regularly, and engage their teachers in conversations about instructional practice are those who are most successful.

Principals must be active partners in creating a rigorous and challenging learning environment. In Chapter Five we will discuss how to mold and shape the culture of your school and make it possible for teachers and other staff to challenge the status quo and modify their practice.

Human Resource Developer

School leaders must also build the capacity of teachers, families, and other school stakeholders. In Chapter Six we'll discuss how to engage these stakeholders in collaborative work to improve the learning of every student.

Skillful leaders work with teachers to ensure that every student is challenged appropriately, that high expectations for student work is evident, and that each classroom provides for the diverse learning styles of students.

They provide support for change initiatives when they work collaboratively to get results with students. Success becomes the motivator and creates the conditions for achieving sustained support.

Change Agent

Providing leadership for any school-wide change is one of the most challenging tasks a school leader will face. Nowhere are the forces of change manifested more dramatically than when the conversation turns to instructional practices and the educational experience of students. Later in this chapter we will discuss strategies for initiating, implementing, and sustaining change in your school.

Change as a Journey, Not an Event

Throughout this book we'll talk about rigor, provide our definition, and discuss the impact on curriculum, instruction, and assessment. We firmly believe that real instructional change, including increasing the rigor of a school's instructional program, begins at the classroom level.

However, school-wide efforts create the climate supportive of these classroom-level changes. We've worked with principals and teachers for more than 20 years. During that time we've seen a variety of ideas designed to improve schools. We've come to appreciate that schools are in a constant state of change. They are shaped by the demographic, social, political, and economic milieu of contemporary American society. As such they change a little each day in response to things like state or national standards, research on student learning, and parent and community demands.

The most successful schools are those that recognize that change is a constant, that improvement is a journey, not an event. Just like a road, the process has multiple paths and you may come unexpectedly upon an intersection and need to change your route. You may find yourself looping back, covering the same stretch of road more than once, or making unplanned stops along the way. Or you may encounter bumps or potholes in the road.

The journey to becoming a more rigorous school is not straight, but winding. To successfully navigate the road it is important to take along a good set of tools—a road map, useful contact information, and a GPS unit or compass.

The BASE Planning Model

After you finish Chapter Two: A Rationale for Rigor, which reviews the challenges and research related to increasing rigor, we'll introduce you to our model for continuous improvement. The BASE planning model describes four critical stages of planning and implementation and will truly serve as a base for the next section: the COMPASS.

BASE Planning Model

- ♦ Begin to Plan
- ♦ Act to Implement
- ♦ Sustain Success
- ♦ Evaluate and Adjust

The COMPASS Model

We find a compass to be a good metaphor for understanding the way that leaders can positively impact rigor in their school. A compass is an incredibly useful tool. It provides direction and guidance. It can help you find your way when lost and can help you stay on track. Most importantly, a compass always remains on target. It stays on "true" north. Our COMPASS sits on the BASE model of planning; overlay the two and you have the toolkit you need for the journey.

C—Creating a Positive and Supportive Culture

We've discovered that to make significant change in a school's program a principal must understand the school's culture and incorporate strategies that will allow them to positively impact the culture.

When we talk about culture, we are talking about the complex set of values, traditions, and patterns of behavior present in a school. A school's culture reflects deeply held beliefs about students and schooling. It manifests itself in "the unwritten rules and assumptions, the combination of rituals and traditions, the array of symbols and artifacts, the special language and phrasing that staff and students use, the expectations for change and learning" (Peterson & Deal, 2002).

Principals recognize the importance of cultural symbols. They use these symbols to promote the institutional values and the school's core mission. Successful principals understand the power of these cultural symbols to telegraph what is important.

Successful principals model the behaviors and practices that they expect others to use. It is important to use constructive language, support risk-taking, and build relationships.

Chapter Five will discuss the importance of culture in more depth and provide strategies and tools that leaders can use to assure a culture supportive of the success of every student.

O—Ownership and Shared Vision

When all the critical stakeholders are engaged in the process, their collective commitment to the change is greater (David, 2009; Hord, 2009). Research also shows that when teachers and others collaborate on instructional issues, their practice changes (Borko, 2004).

When we work with teachers, families, and other school personnel, we almost always find that they have very different ideas about rigor and how it manifests itself in schools. These different ideas about rigor mean that it is important to involve each group in any discussion about increasing rigor in your school.

If your school's mission statement has not been updated in several years, it may be appropriate to review it and make needed changes. Schools change in subtle ways over time. Students are different, the community changes, the economic and social issues change. All of these can lead to changes in a school's mission.

Ownership and shared vision are one of the essential components of our COMPASS model and will be discussed in Chapter Six.

M—Managing Data

Groups that use members' opinions as the primary source of data almost always become contentious. We've found that the most constructive groups are characterized by the gathering and analysis of data independent of any individual's experience or opinion.

It is essential to gather data about student learning. Put together a port-folio of materials that reflect the academic expectations of students, the quality of their work, and the success on agreed upon measures of academic success.

It may also be useful to conduct a self-assessment of your school's program. A brief survey or other instrument can be used to gather data from teachers, parents, students, and others about the rigor of the instructional program. One principal we knew used a simple rubric to assess classroom practices. At a staff meeting groups of teachers worked together to complete the rubric. These data were then used by the School Improvement Team to guide the discussion about the rigor of their program.

Another way to provide data about rigor may be to gather data directly from students. Ron helped a school in Connecticut design an assessment to be completed by students. First, the faculty agreed on their indicators of a rigorous academic program, then a short survey using a Likert scale was constructed. Individual students completed the survey and the results were aggregated by category (grade, gender) to provide information about how students perceived the rigor of their academic program.

These and other strategies will be discussed in Chapter Seven.

P—Professional Development

Also essential to improving rigor in your school's program is providing teachers and other staff with appropriate professional development. The principal can set the direction for a school's professional development agenda. It is important that the principal model a commitment to continuous improvement and be an active participant in professional development activities.

We've found that the most successful professional development is focused on increasing the capacity of the staff. Too often professional development consists of workshops, institutes, or seminars. The most successful models include a wider variety of activities such as collaborative work teams, study groups, critical friends groups, peer coaching, and external support, such as partnerships and networks focused on specific knowledge and skills.

The National Staff Development Council (2001) recommends that professional development focus on improving the learning of all students by organizing adults into learning groups or communities whose goals are aligned with those of the school or district. The groups use disaggregated student data to determine adult learning priorities and sustain improvement, and deepen educators' content knowledge and instructional capacity.

At Tucson High School, Principal Abel Morado organized his staff into a set of small learning communities. Each group, either content or interdisciplinary, selected a goal related to the school's mission and identified data they would collect about their progress. During monthly meetings the work groups reviewed their data, discussed their progress, and identified steps for continued progress. Dr. Morado described the process, "At first they were reluctant. We'd never done anything like this before. So we focused on developing the skills to work together. There's room for improvement, but it is going well. Teachers are talking with one another about students and their learning."

Chapter Eight will explore the importance of professional development in more depth.

A—Advocacy

What leaders pay attention to becomes important (Schein, 2004), and it is important that school leaders are clear about their support for increased rigor. Advocacy is a way to press for changes in your school. It is also a way to build support for your vision of greater rigor and to secure resources to support your vision.

School leaders must advocate with many diverse audiences, both internal and external. They must work with teachers and other staff to assure a shared commitment to greater rigor. They must work with families and community to understand the need for rigor and to cultivate their support. They must also work with district level staff to make sure that their school has the flexibility and resources to support the vision of greater rigor.

One important first step is to build a network with others who share your vision. But don't limit your contact with just those who share your point-of-view. Talk with those who hold other opinions. Monitor your environment. Get to know the "movers and shakers" in your community. Finally, identify your allies and your opponents so that you can build alliances in support of your vision.

Successful advocacy is more than just having a passion for your vision to improve rigor. It requires developing a thoughtful and compelling message about the importance of rigor and identifying strategies to share your vision and mobilize support.

Chapter Nine will provide you with a set of useful tools that you can use to design your advocacy plan and to build support for your vision of a more rigorous school.

S—Shared Accountability

We believe that one of the biggest roadblocks to improving rigor in schools is the resistance from teachers and parents. As we discussed earlier, every person deals differently with change. Some are more accepting; others more resistant.

No change is successful unless accountability is established. We suggest that teachers, families, and community along with school leaders are accountable for increasing rigor.

Accountability is more than issuing mandates and forcing compliance. For school leaders it involves energizing and motivating individuals as well as groups.

As we discussed earlier, the culture of the school must be one where high value is placed on improving students' educational experience, where there is a collective commitment to improvement, and a parallel commitment to supporting people who take risks and make changes. Further, the culture must not accept failure as an option. Every student must be expected to learn and the staff must be committed to supporting students in their learning.

The most important role of a school leader is as instructional leader. But the principal is not the only person responsible for a quality instructional program. Teachers and other staff are responsible for delivering instruction and positively impacting every student's learning.

School leaders, however, are responsible for creating a climate and culture at their school that supports quality instruction, promotes innovation, and nurtures professional growth. You can do this by:

- providing time for collegial discussion and dialogue about improved instruction, including time to reflect on efforts to improve rigor;
- staying current on educational trends and developments;
- modeling quality instructional practices at meetings and during other interaction with staff; and
- attending and actively participating in professional development and other learning opportunities.

Shared accountability is critical to your efforts to improve rigor. Chapter Ten will discuss the issue in more depth and provide additional ideas that you can use in your school to build a collective commitment to the success of every student.

S—Structures

The day-to-day routines and structures of your school can impact your ability to become more rigorous. Structures, frequently rooted in past practice, can be major barriers to reform or they can be used to accelerate achieving your vision of a more rigorous school.

In many schools the most significant structural barrier is the isolation of teachers from one another. Many schools have created professional learning communities (PLC). While PLC's take many forms, they almost always focus on student learning and value time for teachers and administrators to work together to talk about student learning and decide how to improve their school.

The design of the school's schedule is another important structural factor. Designing a schedule to provide collaborative time, to organize teachers into collaborative instructional groups, and to provide students with opportunities to receive extra support are essential.

School policies and practices, such as homework and grading procedures, also shape your vision of a more rigorous school.

Structures that can support your efforts to become a more rigorous school will be examined in Chapter Eleven. It is the final element of our COMPASS model.

Getting Started

People respond to change in many different ways. That is especially true when the conversation deals with rigor in schools.

We once heard a speaker compare the impact of change to crossing a busy street on a foggy day. Before any change, people are on the cement curb on one side of the street. They know that once they get to the other side they will once again be standing on a solid cement curb. The difficulty is that people must step away from the safety of the curb they know, walk into a foggy street, and be confident that they will successfully get to the other side.

The leader's role is to help people navigate foggy streets, to provide the confidence that the future will be secure, and to assure that people will be supported throughout the change.

Check Your Own Assumptions

We all hold assumptions about things. Those assumptions are based on our experiences and reflect our own idiosyncratic experiences. In any group, its members bring to the conversation their own assumptions.

What Assumptions Do You Hold?

- ◆ What do you believe about rigor?
- ◆ What motivation strategies work most successfully with your school community?
- ◆ How quickly do you believe your school can become more rigorous?
- ◆ What conditions are most likely to result in a more rigorous school?
- ◆ Is your vision of rigor the one that should be implemented?

Most organizations, including schools, resist change. You've probably heard many of these before. They are often used to justify keeping things the way they are. "Let sleeping dogs lie." "If it ain't broke, don't fix it." "Just wait a couple of years and this principal (superintendent) will be gone." "We tried it once before and it didn't work."

Schools are increasingly expected to assume greater responsibility for helping students adapt, and indeed thrive, in a changing world. This means you need to examine the very essence of your school, your core beliefs, and how they impact teaching and learning.

Over the years we've learned a lot about how schools change. We've learned that key stakeholders must be involved. We know that it almost always involves conflict and disagreement, and that real change takes time and sustained effort.

The Leader and Change

- Effective change takes time. It is a process of development and requires persistence.
- The complexity of change means that everyone may not agree on what is proposed.
- Conflict and disagreement are part of the process and help to clarify beliefs and next steps. They are fundamental to successful change.
- Any significant change requires those implementing the change to be involved and make their own meaning.
- The lack of implementation may not be rejection of the change. It may be lack of time or other resources.
- Change is really about changing the culture of your school.
- People respond best when conditions allow them to react to ideas, form their own position, interact with others, and be provided with professional development and other technical assistance.

Adapted from: Fullan, 2001a, 2001b; Glickman et al., 2001

Use Positive and Supportive Leadership Behaviors

Successful principals model the behaviors and practices that they expect others to use. It is important to use constructive language, support risk-taking, and build relationships.

We've found that when principals talk with teachers and other staff about instructional issues like rigor it is valuable to use language and practices that open the communication rather than close it. In particular, we've found the following characterize constructive group dynamics:

- ♦ Listen, don't get defensive
- ♦ Ask questions, don't accuse
- ♦ Respect the complexity of change; don't expect immediate results
- ♦ Value different points-of-view; don't tell people what to believe
- ♦ Value collaboration; don't expect agreement on everything
- ♦ Trust people to do the right thing; don't demand compliance

It is important that leaders be active and engaged learners, that they demonstrate their support for any instructional change.

Final Thoughts

Most changes in schools take place in response to events (different students, societal trends). These events help to identify a need. Schools respond to these emerging needs in one of three ways—ignore them, reject them, or address them.

A starkly different approach is a much more thoughtful and deliberative planning process. We suggest that when you work with your community to increase rigor it is best to use a deliberative process, one that involves important stakeholders, provides for discussion about approaches and strategies, utilizes a collaborative approach to making decisions, regularly collects data about progress, and develops capacity to sustain the work.

Before you move any further in *Rigorous Schools and Classrooms*, we'd like to ask you to stop and think about your vision for a rigorous school. If your school, classroom, or district were truly rigorous, what would that look like? How would your teachers and students be different? What would you be doing differently than you are today? Take a few moments, sit down with a blank sheet of paper, and sketch out your vision—either in narrative, bullet points, or diagrams. Then hold onto it, we'll come back to this at the end of the book.

2

A Rationale for Rigor

Concern about rigor is not new. Since the release of *A Nation at Risk* (National Commission on Excellence in Education, 1983), the debate about the quality of America's schools has grown exponentially. This debate calls for dramatically different schools—schools that are much more responsive to student need and provide a rigorous curriculum that prepares students for success in higher education and the workplace.

Adoption of *No Child Left Behind* in 2001 raised the debate to a new level. For the first time, schools would be held accountable for the achievement of every student, not just the most capable.

For over 20 years we've worked with teachers and principals on ways to improve their schools. Our efforts have centered on creating schools where every student is known by adults, has a positive relationship with adults and other students, and where every student is challenged to achieve at high levels.

Throughout the nation the 3 R's—Rigor, Relevance, and Relationships—are now accepted as necessary characteristics of schools. Many states have adopted the 3 R's model as a requirement for school improvement efforts.

Myths About Rigor

As we work with schools, we've met thousands of committed teachers and principals. Together they work incredibly hard to positively impact the learning of every student. At the same time as we've talked abut changing instruction, adding rigor to schools and classrooms, and providing greater support for student success, we've come to recognize several myths that cloud the conversation of rigor.

> ### *Myths About Rigor*
> ◆ Lots of Homework Is a Sign of Rigor
> ◆ Rigor Means Doing More
> ◆ Rigor is Not for Everyone
> ◆ Providing Support Means Lessening Rigor

Myth #1: Lots of Homework Is a Sign of Rigor

For many people there is probably no more prevalent indicator of rigor that the amount of homework required of students (Jackson, 2009). Many teachers pride themselves on the amount of homework expected of their students.

The dilemma is that all homework is not equally useful. Some of it is just busywork, assigned by teachers because principals or parents expect it. Too often, "difficulty is often equated to the amount of work done by students, rather than the complexity and challenge" (Williamson & Johnston, 1999, p. 10).

One study (Wasserstein, 1995) found that students described busywork as unimportant, and therefore, not satisfying. Contrary to what many adults believe, the study found that students viewed hard work as important and enjoyed the challenge and enjoyment that went with accomplishing a task that was hard.

Vatterott (2009) found that homework is often built on the misconceived idea that doing more of something must mean more learning. The "more is better" idea permeates the discussion of rigor.

Dick Flanary of the National Association of Secondary School Principals described the impact, "Too often, rigor becomes 'Let's give more homework. Lessons must be 'rigorous' if they make kids suffer'" (Hechinger, 2009, p. 3).

"Doing more" often means doing more low-level activities, frequently repetitions of things already learned. Such narrow and rigid approaches to learning do not define a rigorous classroom.

Students learn in many different ways. Just as instruction must vary to meet the individual needs of students, so must homework. Rigorous and challenging learning experiences will vary with the student. Their design will vary, as will their duration.

Myth #2: Rigor Means Doing More

Many parents and educators believe that a rigorous classroom is characterized by requiring students to do more than they currently do, that rigor is defined by the content of a lesson, the amount of reading, the volume of homework, or the number of assignments.

Rigor is more than just content and cannot be measured by the amount of things students must do. Tony Wagner (2008a) studied classrooms across America and found that many of them were characterized by low-level, rote activity. The focus was too often on covering material or preparation for the next test.

A few years ago Ron and Howard Johnston conducted a study to find out how teachers and parents defined rigor. What they found was that the two groups held startlingly different definitions. Teachers said that rigor meant doing more work while parents said that rigor was doing less but more in-depth.

The challenge for school leaders is how to reconcile these differences and work with teachers, parents, and community to develop a shared vision for a rigorous school and to mobilize resources in support of improved rigor.

True rigor is expecting every student to learn and perform at high levels. This requires instruction that allows students to delve deeply into their learning, to engage in critical thinking and problem solving activities, to be curious and imaginative, and to demonstrate agility and adaptability (Wagner, 2008a).

Myth #3: Rigor is Not for Everyone

There is a belief that the only way to assure success for everyone is to lower standards and lessen rigor. Such beliefs often mask an underlying belief that some students are less capable and that their success will hold back those that are more capable.

There is growing recognition that all students must be provided an opportunity for a rigorous educational experience. Michigan recently revised its requirements for a high school diploma. All students must now complete three and a half years of mathematics, including Algebra II and Geometry, as well Biology and either Chemistry or Physics. The expectation is that schools will design networks of support to ensure that every student is successful.

Rigor, however, is more than a set of courses. It is anchored in the belief that every student can be successful given adequate time and sufficient support. Tony Wagner (2008b) suggests that our society's success rests on a commitment to providing every student with a set of skills that will allow them to become "productive citizens who contribute to solving some of the most pressing issues we face" (p. 21) and who thrive in a collaborative environment.

The National High School Alliance suggests that a "rigor agenda" must assure that every student, not just the traditionally college-bound, is well prepared for post-secondary education, a career, and participation in civic life. Ultimately, the Alliance suggests, it is about improving student achievement, for every student.

There is no evidence that supporting the success of every student means lessening rigor or the quality of schools. Just the opposite, it demonstrates our shared commitment to a more equitable and just society, one where every student has the skills for life-long success.

Myth #4: Providing Support Means Lessening Rigor

A belief central to the American psyche is that of rugged individualism—do things on your own. Working in teams or with support is often seen as a sign of weakness.

We've found that supporting students so that they can learn at high levels (Blackburn, 2008) is central to the definition of rigor. As teachers design lessons moving students toward more challenging work they must provide scaffolding to support them as they learn.

When Ron and Howard conducted their study, they asked teachers and parents about their experience with rigor. Both groups repeatedly told stories of how successful they were on rigorous tasks when they felt a high level of support, a safety net. Often people described tasks that were initially not successful. Only after additional time or effort did they experience success. In fact, many people said that they would not have been successful without strong support.

The same is true for students. They are motivated to do well when they value what they are doing and when they believe that they have a chance of success. The most successful schools are those that build a culture of success, celebrate success, and build a success mentality.

The Call for Rigor

Demands for a more rigorous educational experience continue. Almost every year a report is issued suggesting how America's schools can become more rigorous.

Greater rigor in schools has struck a chord with families of children in our schools. Those families are bombarded with information suggesting the knowledge and skills their children will need for success. Recent changes in the American economy have accelerated family interest in assuring that their children receive a rigorous curriculum.

Reports on Rigor	
Research Findings	*Source(s)*
Many high school graduates are unprepared for college	Achieve (2007); Williamson (2006)
Too few high school graduates are getting needed skills and are taking remediation courses in college	ACT (2007); Achieve (2007); American Diploma Project (n.d.); Dyer (n.d.); United States Department of Education as cited in Williamson (2006)
College readiness translates into work readiness as well	ACT (2007)
Employers say that high school graduates are lacking basic skills	American Diploma Project (n.d.); Williamson (2006)
Students planning to join the workforce after graduation do not need a less rigorous curriculum—they need higher order thinking skills	American Diploma Project (n.d.); Cavanagh (2004); National High School Alliance (2006a)
Students are not prepared for high school	ACT (2007)

Concern about rigor, however, is not limited to underperforming schools. Recently Tony Wagner (2008), Co-Director of the Change Leadership Group at the Harvard Graduate School of Education, questioned the academic rigor of even our "best schools." He visited dozens of classrooms and observed students and teachers at work. He found that far too often students in honors and advanced placement (AP) classes were engaged in low-level instructional activities where students were not expected to use higher order thinking skills. Wagner reported that "Of the hundreds of classes that I've observed in recent years, fewer than 1 in 20 were engaged in instruction designed to teach students to think instead of merely drilling for the test" (p. 24).

After talking with a group of the nation's top business leaders, from places like Apple, Unilever, and the U.S. Army, Wagner identified seven skills that every student must master in order to survive in the 21st century.

Survival Skills for the 21st Century

1. Critical Thinking and Problem Solving
2. Collaboration and Leadership
3. Agility and Adaptability
4. Initiative and Entrepreneurialism
5. Effective Oral and Written Communication
6. Accessing and Analyzing Information
7. Curiosity and Imagination

From: Wagner (2008a)

More Recent Discussion of Rigor

Since Barbara began writing *Rigor is Not a Four-Letter Word* (2008), several reports addressing rigor have been released. The first, *Reading Between the Lines* (2006) from ACT concluded that most high school students are not prepared for college level reading. That was no surprise to us since we both work in higher education and are faced with students who occasionally lack the reading and writing skills for success in college.

A second report was published the same year. *The Silent Epidemic: Perspectives of High School Drop-Outs* (2006) reported on the experience of high school dropouts and surprised many by revealing that 88% of those who dropped out were not failing school, and that 70% of the dropouts believed they could have graduated.

So, what went wrong? Students reported that they were not expected to work hard (66%) and/or were not motivated (69%). They also reported that classes weren't interesting (47%). Perhaps most surprisingly, two-thirds of the students said they would have worked harder if more had been demanded from them.

Before we discount their beliefs, those same students shared strong views about how to improve their educational experience.

The comments from these dropouts are similar to those reported in other studies. A recent *ASCD Smart Brief* described a study conducted in low-performing schools in Newark, NJ (Yeung, 2009) where it was found that allowing students to struggle with challenging math problems led to improved achievement and results on standardized tests. A "healthy amount of frustration" was described by the study as healthy and that this contributed to student satisfaction with having struggled and succeeded on the tasks.

This study affirms earlier work by Wasserstein (1995) in his study of middle school students and schoolwork. Students reported that they equated hard work with success and satisfaction. But, they also said that "hard work" was important work and should be done. Assignments that were not "hard or challenging" were unimportant and, therefore, less likely to be completed.

Wasserstein also found that students did not turn away from challenging work but instead craved it. Students reported that their self-esteem was enhanced when they accomplished something they thought might be beyond them. Interestingly, Wasserstein also found that students of all abilities and backgrounds craved doing important work and had a disdain for busywork.

Early in 2009, the Hechinger Institute released its report on academic rigor in schools. The report, a collection of articles by noted researchers, teachers, and laypeople, identified advantages to rigorous learning but also noted that "the 'content vs. critical thinking' debate is a false dichotomy" (p. 23). It suggests that both approaches are complementary, not exclusive.

The report suggests that rigor has become a "buzz word" with little meaning academically" (p. 1). The debate over rigor reflects America's continuing "tension between the ideals of academic excellence and universal access to education" (p. 1).

Many suggest that a more rigorous education is the solution to our industrial malaise, the solution to an underprepared workforce, and a necessity for our future. Sadly, the report concluded that rigor has become a marketing tool promising all sorts of benefits from increasing self-esteem to assuring admission to preferred colleges.

The National High School Alliance (2006a; 2006b), a partnership of fifty organizations committed to high academic achievement, released a pair of reports examining rigor in American high schools. They identified four core principles of a school with a rigorous program.

Core Principles

+ Minimum graduation requirements that prepare students for college
+ High level content and instruction
+ Wide range of supports for students to help them succeed
+ Alignment of requirements with post-secondary education and work

---

Most importantly, the Alliance said that a single focus on course titles is not sufficient. "Efforts to increase rigor also require careful examination of course content to ensure it is at an appropriately high level, and teaches students higher order thinking skills" (National High School Alliance, 2006b, p. 3). Other efforts recommended by the Alliance include improved guidance and counseling, individualization and personalization, academic supports for struggling students, and substantial investment in professional development and other teacher supports.

Two Million Minutes, a short but powerful documentary produced by a PBS station and available on YouTube and other sites (www.2mminutes.com) has caught the attention of many educators. It suggests that as a student completes eighth grade that student has about two million minutes until high school graduation—two million minutes that will affect the rest of their lives. It questions how students spend that time and what schools can do to assure every student completes high school with the knowledge, skills, and dispositions for success.

A recent ACT report, *The Forgotten Middle* (2008), found that few eighth-graders were on track for college-level work when they graduate from high school. Those on track were prepared for success in both high school and beyond.

The ACT report identifies the most important factors for student success in college. They include both a record of academic success but also academic discipline including attitudes about school, about attendance, and about completion of assignments.

The implications of the report affirm the need to intervene with students long before they reach high school if we are going to build a culture of success. A key recommendation is that kindergarten through eighth grade focus on essential college readiness skills and that they should be nonnegotiable for every student. Further the report suggests that every student be monitored and that interventions occur when students fall of track or are not on target.

Beginning the Work on an Agenda of Rigor

The longer we work with teachers and principals, the more we believe we have to move beyond debate about the rhetoric about rigor—the charges and countercharges. We need to focus on how to positively impact every student we teach in a way that increases their learning and creates the capacity to be a vibrant, contributing citizen.

A friend of ours, Karen Hickman, from Texas said it directly. We need to move toward "implementation of rigor instead of so much talk about it!"

Later in the book we will discuss specific planning ideas and will share a set of tools that we find useful in beginning the work on rigor. We'll also talk about resistance and how to overcome it and built support among teachers and families for a more rigorous program.

For now, we want to briefly describe three questions that must be addressed if you are going to make progress.

Three Questions

- ♦ What Does It Mean?
- ♦ How Do I Get There?
- ♦ Where Do I Go From Here?

What Does It Mean?

In his commentary *Rigor on Trial*, Tony Wagner (2006) comments that there is "no common agreement on what constitutes rigor." ACT (2009) in its recent report on rigor offered more than a dozen different definitions of rigor. The following illustrate the varied points-of-view.

Definitions of Rigor	
Quality of thinking, not quantity, and that can occur in any grade and at any subject	Bogess (2007)
High expectations are important and must include effort on the part of the learner	Wasley, Hampel, and Clark (1997)
Deep immersion in a subject and should include real-world settings and working with an expert	Washor and Mojkowki (2006)
"'Rigor' would be used to say something about how an experience or activity is carried out and to what degree. Specifically, a 'rigorous' experience would be one that involves depth and care as, for example, in a scientific experiment or literary analysis that is done thoughtfully, deeply with sufficient depth and attention to accuracy and detail."	Beane (2001)

"Goal of helping students develop the capacity to understand content that is complex, ambiguous, provocative, and personally or emotionally challenging."	Strong, Silver, and Perrini (2001, p. 7)
Rigor for the 21st century includes a focus on skills for life: critical thinking and problem solving, collaboration and leadership, agility and adaptability, initiative and entrepreneurialism, effective oral and written communication, accessing and analyzing information, and curiosity and imagination.	Wagner (2008)
"Rigor quite simply means giving students a curriculum that will prepare them to succeed in college or the world of work. For us, that means setting a high standard for success and then lining up each grade's lessons to meet that high standard."	Weast (in Hechinger Institute, 2009)
"Academic rigor means raising the bar, elevating expectations and increasing the level of challenge . . . for our children. It also means changing our expectations. . . . We need to have the mindset that all of our children must go to college or get technical training to be prepared for 21st century jobs."	Granholm (in Hechinger Institute, 2009)

Beyond the debate about the definition of rigor we recognize that rigor is more about a process, a way of thinking, involving depth and thought. It is also about the content that is being taught and the design of the lesson, the support provided students, and the expectation that every student will be successful.

How to Get There?

So, how do you get started on creating a culture of rigor in your school? The journey is shaped by how people define rigor. Beyond the definitions provided earlier we think that rigor is about course content, assessments, and relationships.

Courses and Course Content

Recommendations About Courses/Course Content	
Expand access to high quality courses	ACT (2007; 2008); National High School Alliance (2006)
Improve the quality and content of the core academic areas	ACT (2007; 2008); Cavanagh (2004)
States should specify course content	Hechinger Institute (2009); ACT (2008); American Diploma Project (n.d.)
Specify the number and kinds of courses that students should take for graduation	ACT (2007; 2008)
Raise graduation requirements	Hechinger Institute (2009); National High School Alliance (2006); American Diploma Project (n.d.)

There is research to support the belief that the College Board's Advanced Placement (AP) courses are beneficial, particularly in terms of success in college (http://www.washingtonpost.com/wp-dyn/content/article/2007/01/28/AR2007012801238.html), but the AP program has its critics. A recent report, *Growing Pains in Advanced Placement Programs* (Fordham Institute, 2009) found AP teachers divided about whether AP courses should be offered to all interested students or only those with demonstrated ability.

The discussion about rigor, though, is about more than particular courses. Often, the measure of rigor is state standards. Almost all state assessments, however, measure low levels of student achievement when compared to the National Assessment of Educational Progress (NAEP, 2007).

There are many sets of standards that provide helpful comparisons to national standards. One of our favorites is the benchmark guidelines and rubrics based on NAEP and developed by the Southern Regional Education Board (http://www.sreb.org). Other standards include the New Standards Performance Standards (1997) developed by The National Center on Education and the Economy (http://www.ncee.org). These standards are for English/Language Arts, Mathematics, Science, and Applied Learning.

Recently the National Governors Association Center for Best Practices and the Council of Chief State School Officers launched *The Common Core State Standards Initiative*. The initiative (http://www.corestandards.org) is designed to develop a common set of standards in English-Language Arts and in Mathematics from grades K-12. The first set of draft standards was released for review in the fall of 2009.

Another set of useful standards are the SCANS standards (Secretary's Commission on Achieving Necessary Skills, 1992). The standards (http://wdr.doleta.gov/SCANS/) identified the skills young people need to be successful in the world of work. The standards continue to be a useful source of information about the skills needed to work in today's economic environment.

Assessments

Another way to increase rigor is to examine assessments. We know the importance of assessments and will talk more about them later in the book. However, a review of the research on rigor makes it clear that we need assessments that have variety, re-enforce the value of learning, and are motivating. Assessments that merely ask students to regurgitate content or facts do not promote an agenda of rigor.

Recommendations About Assessments	
Use a variety of assessments	American Diploma Project (n.d.); Washor & Mojkowski (2006); Hechinger Institute (2009)
Provide relevant assessments	Daggett (2005); Dyer (n.d.)
Assess processes, techniques, exhibitions, and project reports	Washor & Mojkowski(2006)

Recommendations About Assessments (continued)	
K-12 and higher education should collaborate on assessments and vertical alignment	Achieve (2007)
Measure results at a course level	ACT (2007)

Teacher/Student Interaction and Support

The third area is the importance of designing lessons that are relevant, require students to use high-level skills, and build positive relationships with students—relationships built on a commitment to student success and that provide the support for students to achieve at high levels.

Recommendations About Teacher/Student Interaction and Support	
Students and teachers should be reflective	Bogess (2007); Washor & Mojkowski (2006)
Work in a close setting	National High School Alliance (2006); Washor & Mojkowski (2006)
Learning connected to student interests	National High School Alliance (2006); Southern Regional Education Board (2004); Washor & Mojkowski(2006)
Connect learning to real world contexts	National High School Alliance (2006); Southern Regional Education Board (2004); Dyer (n.d.); Washor & Mojkowski (2006)
Build relationships with students	Southern Regional Education Board (2004); Washor & Mojkowski (2006)

Related Issues

Of course there are a variety of other issues schools face in addition to rigor. Schools are working on many different initiatives to improve their educational program. There are several that we've identified that support an agenda to improve rigor.

Research on Related Issues	
Small learning communities engaged in reflective thought with high expectations that lead to success	Hord & Sommers (2008); Kohm & Nance (2007); Reeves (2009)
Integrate nonacademic subjects, such as physical education, music, art, with academic standards to improve instruction	Reeves (2003)
Highly qualified teachers should be assigned to students who need them the most	ACT (2007; 2009); California Gear Up (www.castategearup. org)
Teachers need support	ACT (2007; 2009); Southern Regional Education Board (2004)

We recognize that the discussion of rigor includes even more issues like school or class size, interdisciplinary teaching, teacher quality, and professional development.

Where Do I Go From Here?

We believe that real change, change that impacts every student, occurs at the classroom level. The power of every teacher, working with committed colleagues, can make a difference for students.

Our intent is not to offer another program or suggest another policy. It is to provide practical tools that every leader can use to positively impact their school. There is no silver bullet, no single program or directive that can increase rigor in your school.

But we've found that in classrooms where all students learn, regardless of gender, ethnicity, poverty level, or background, teachers and leaders do two things. They care deeply about their students. Building a strong relationship with students is important, but not enough. You also have to care enough to work with every student to assure that they rise to higher levels. We have come to recognize that rigor is not just about what is taught or the classes that students take. It is all about expectations, instructional effectiveness, and assessment practices.

> *Rigor is ensuring that each student is provided the opportunity to grow in ways they cannot imagine.*

So, how do we make sense of the research on rigor? Barbara developed a definition of rigor that we believe incorporates the most important characteristics (Blackburn, 2008). We will use this definition as we share with you strategies that we've learned promote an agenda of rigor.

Definition of Rigor

Rigor is creating an environment in which each student is expected to learn at high levels, each student is supported so he or she can learn at high levels, and each student demonstrates learning at high levels.

Throughout the book we will focus on how all school leaders, not just principals, work with teachers, families, and community to build a culture of rigor and to assure a quality learning experience for every student.

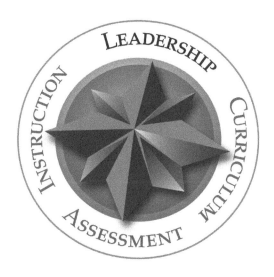

3

Recognizing Rigor

> Rigor is creating an environment in which each student is expected to learn at high levels, each student is supported so he or she can learn at high levels, and each student demonstrates learning at high levels (Blackburn, 2008).

In Chapter Two, *The Rationale for Rigor*, we introduced Barbara's definition of rigor: creating an environment in which each student is expected to learn at high levels, each student is supported so he or she can learn at high levels, and each student demonstrates learning at high levels. Notice we are looking at the environment you create. Our tri-fold approach to rigor is not limited to the curriculum students are expected to learn. It is more than a specific lesson or instructional strategy. It is deeper than what a student says or does in response to a lesson. True rigor is the result of weaving together all elements of schooling to raise students to higher levels of learning.

On the following pages, you'll find a rubric that describes the varying components of rigor.

Rubric for Gauging Progress Toward Rigor

	Starting at the Base	Making Progress Up the Mountain	Reaching New Heights
High Expectations for Learning	I am working to understand what it means to say that each student can learn, will learn, and I will help them do so.	I believe that each student can learn, will learn, and I will help them do so. I sometimes act on those beliefs or I act on those beliefs with some students.	I consistently act on my unwavering belief that each student can learn, will learn, and I will help them do so.
Support and Scaffolding	I sometimes provide support and scaffolding. This support is usually general and built into the regular lesson. At times, I provide optional extra help.	I sometimes provide the appropriate support and scaffolding students need to ensure their success. This support is customized for each student at times. At times, I provide optional extra help.	I regularly provide the support and scaffolding each student needs to ensure their success. This support is customized for each student and supports my belief that students are not allowed to not learn. It is appropriate and encourages independence. If extra help is needed, it is required, and is offered when the student can attend.

Continues on next page.

Rubric for Gauging Progress Toward Rigor (cont'd)

	Starting at the Base	Making Progress Up the Mountain	Reaching New Heights
Demonstration of Learning	Occasionally, some students demonstrate understanding of content in a way that is appropriately challenging. More often than not, students prefer basic assignments or questions. Students are generally given one opportunity to show they have mastered content.	Sometimes, students are given the opportunity to show they understand content in a way that is appropriately challenging. Students are beginning to see the value of more challenging assessments. At times, I provide alternative assessments and will allow students to redo work.	Each student regularly demonstrates their understanding of content in ways that are appropriately challenging. In other words, students do not take the easy way out in terms of showing me they learned. I provide alternative ways for students to do this and allow those students who need it extra time or a second opportunity.

Continues on next page.

Rubric for Gauging Progress Toward Rigor (cont'd)

	Starting at the Base	Making Progress Up the Mountain	Reaching New Heights
Level of Student Engagement	There are limited opportunities for students to be engaged in learning beyond listening and taking notes. Most of my instruction is directed toward the whole class. At times, I provide the opportunity for students to work with another student to apply their learning.	Some students are actively engaged in learning. There is a mix of whole group and small group/partner activities, and some activities are interactive. I facilitate some activities, and some ownership is shifted to students. However, the focus is still on me.	All students are actively engaged in learning. Each is participating in every aspect of the lesson by making connections, contributing to the discussion (whether small group, partner, or whole group), and responding to learning. The majority of the activities are interactive, and whole group activities are limited. I am the facilitator, and the focus for learning is on the students.
Motivational Element: Value	I ask students to apply my lessons to their real lives. I make sure my students understand how my lesson applies to future tests they will take (such as standardized testing). I sometimes share with them why I think the content is important.	I sometimes design lessons that allow students to see the value. I incorporate real-life application activities into some of my lessons. If they volunteer, students can share their own applications of learning.	I design lessons that allow students to see the value of the specific learning. Application activities are woven seamlessly throughout the lesson. Students are given ample opportunity to make personal connections about relevance to their own lives and futures.

Continues on next page.

Rubric for Gauging Progress Toward Rigor (cont'd)

	Starting at the Base	*Making Progress Up the Mountain*	*Reaching New Heights*
Motivational Element: Success	If the majority of my students aren't learning, I reteach the content of the lesson. Sometimes, I provide opportunities for students to come in for extra help if they want to. I expect my students to succeed, and I am learning how to help them understand that.	I build scaffolding into some lessons. I provide opportunities for students to come in for extra help when needed. I regularly tell my students that I expect them to succeed, and I try to help them make that a reality.	I build appropriate scaffolding and support into every lesson. Students know my focus is to remove barriers to their success. I require students to come in for extra help when needed, and I support them in positive ways that encourage growth and independent learning. All students know that we learn together, and that they can be successful.
Overall Classroom Culture	Members of our learning community (students, teachers, parents, etc.) are learning what it means to set a standard that **not learning** is unacceptable. We are also discussing how to move beyond grades to authentic learning. We celebrate some of our successes.	Some members of our learning community (students, teachers, parents, etc.) believe that it is unacceptable **to not learn.** We are learning to focus on learning in addition to grades. We celebrate success as well as progress.	Every member of our learning community (students, teachers, parents, etc.) believes that it is unacceptable **to not learn.** The focus is on learning at high levels, not just grades. We celebrate success as well as progress.

It was originally introduced in *Rigor is NOT a Four-Letter Word* to be used as a general tool and a starting point for discussions about rigor. The next step, however, is one of the questions we hear most often from school leaders. "Tell me what that looks like in a real classroom."

Expecting Students to Learn at High Levels

So, let's look at this definition in more detail. First, rigor is *creating an environment in which each student is expected to learn at high levels.* Having high expectations starts with the decision that every student has the potential to be his or her best, no matter what. There are times this is hard, but we've always remembered that students live up to or down to our level of expectation for them. When Barbara was a teacher, she worked with a student who came into her classroom with a reputation as a poor student and troublemaker. Despite her efforts, it was difficult to move past her preconceived notions of his work. As she began to work with him, it was evident that he had potential, but she had to let go of her expectations of him based on her prior knowledge.

This is a common problem. Almost everyone we talk with says "we have high expectations for our students." Sometimes that is evidenced by the behaviors in the school; at other times actions do not necessarily match the words. What exactly are concrete ways to show you have high expectations for students? There are three key areas: challenging curriculum, high levels of instruction, and teacher behaviors.

Characteristics of Expecting Students to Learn at High Levels

- ◆ Challenging Curriculum
- ◆ High Levels of Instruction
- ◆ Adult Behaviors

Challenging Curriculum

Barbara was at a middle school in Maryland and had a conversation with Gabrielle, a student at the school. Our favorite question to ask students is, "If you were in charge of the school, what would you change?" Her answer was insightful. She said, "For people who don't understand much . . . [they should] be in higher level classes to understand more [because] if they already don't know much, you don't want to teach them to not know much over and over." Isn't that reflective of how students view our levels of classes when some are not labeled "high level?"

In Chapter Three of *Rigor is NOT a Four-Letter Word*, Barbara provides a thorough process for evaluating curriculum against outside standards. She follows this with a discussion of teachers simply comparing their own expectations to develop consistency. Here's a tool you can ask your teachers to use to look at their standards and expectations.

Standards or Expectations	*Comparison*
Standard/Assignment	Comparison to Benchmarks:
Assignment	Comparison of assessment with other teachers:
Expectations	What I learned from teachers a grade higher:
Expectations	What I learned from teachers a grade lower:
What I want to do with the new information I learned:	

High Levels of Instruction

Next, we need to look at how curriculum is taught. As you work with teachers to create and adapt lessons to incorporate more rigorous opportunities for learning, you will need to consider the questions that are embedded within instruction. We recently talked with a teacher who was using higher standards and more complex activities, but she asked her students basic recall or memory-based questions to assess their understanding. That defeats the purpose. Higher-level questioning is an integral part of a rigorous classroom. Look for open-ended questions, ones that are at the higher levels of Bloom's Taxonomy.

However, it's also important to look at how teachers respond to questions. We often provide "rigor audits" for schools, which are outside views of the level of rigor in the school. In a recent school visit with walkthroughs designed to provide an overall picture of the school, Barbara noticed that even if teachers asked higher level questions, they accepted low-level answers from students. At times, teachers would cut students off from answering and then answer the question themselves. In a rigorous classroom, teachers push students to respond at high levels, often asking extending questions. If a student does not know the answer, the teacher continues to probe and guide the student to an answer rather than simply moving on to the next student.

As you visit classrooms, you can use a simple tally tool to chart your observations about questioning techniques. Then, you can look for overall patterns as part of your data set.

Tally Tool		
	Low Level/Rote	*High Level/ Application*
Questions Asked		
	Low Level Response Accepted	*High Level Response or Probing/Extending Questions*
Response from Teacher after Student's Response		

Another critical aspect of instruction is limiting the amount of review, or reviewing content in a new manner. Since our focus in this book is leadership behaviors, we will not spend time describing step-by-step how to teach lessons; you will find that information in *Rigor is NOT a Four Letter Word* (see

Chapter Three). But, as a leader, look for the amount of time spent on review. In a recent classroom visit to an honors English class, students were writing notes about nouns (a noun is a person, place, thing, or idea). Then, they underlined nouns in a passage on a worksheet. The teacher explained that students still did not understand nouns. We understand, but finding more application-oriented writing activities is a more rigorous way to review. After all, if underlining nouns in a sentence truly worked for these students, they would understand nouns prior to honors English.

A final strategy is to simply incorporate simple activities that are more rigorous. For example, many teachers use the pair-share strategy of having students turn to a partner and share an answer to a question. Then, the teacher typically calls on one or two students to share their responses. We raise that a level by asking students to share their partner's responses. In doing so, students are more attentive to their partner during the pair-share, and they learn the importance of listening for understanding.

Adult Behaviors

Finally, teachers and leaders can demonstrate higher expectations through specific behaviors. The first of these is our choice of language that is allowed and used. In her early days of teaching, Barbara found that her at-risk students continually used the phrase "I Can't." No matter the task, their default response was, "I can't do that." After she implemented a system in which that was not allowed, her students realized that they were expected to at least try each task. Over time, they were more successful in learning.

Alternatives to the Phrase "I Can't"

- ◆ I'll try.
- ◆ I'm not sure how, so I need help.
- ◆ I don't understand. Would you explain it in a different way?
- ◆ What do I need to do first?

A second consideration is language and how our words impact students. As adults, our words have tremendous power. Especially when we are asking our students to move to higher levels of learning, they need encouragement. Our words and actions either encourage or discourage.

We cannot underestimate the power of the words we choose. Sometimes when we're frustrated we choose harsh language in order to convey our frustration. Or we may use encouraging words but in a way that conveys our unhappiness. Always think about the words you use because the words, and the tone in which they are delivered, send unspoken messages to people about your beliefs.

Examples of Adult Language	
Encouraging Statements	*Discouraging Statements*
I know this seems hard, but I also know you can do it. It looks difficult, but you've done this before (insert example). You can do it again. If you need extra help, I'm here for you.	I know this will be too hard for most of you. I know you don't understand, but do the homework anyway. I've already explained that enough

Finally, the use of appropriate wait time is critical. During our classroom visits, we notice several trends related to wait time. First, wait time for students to answer is usually very limited. This may be due to the pressure teachers feel to "cover the material," their concern over student embarrassment, or discomfort with silence. No matter the reason, often students are not given time to process learning before they are asked to respond. We also notice a pattern that in general, students in honors or advanced classes are given more wait time. Third, often times, even when students provide an answer that is not the exact answer the teacher wants, they are cut off, even in midsentence, or the teacher moves to another student.

Supporting Students to Learn at High Levels

Supporting Each Student to Learn at High Levels
- ◆ Scaffolding Within Lessons
- ◆ Incorporating Motivation
- ◆ Addressing Strategic Knowledge
- ◆ Providing Extra Help

The strategies we just discussed directly impact the second part of our definition: *each student is supported so he or she can learn at high levels*. It is critical that teachers craft lessons that move students to more challenging work while simultaneously providing ongoing scaffolding to support them as they learn. We simply cannot increase our expectations without helping students learn to move with us to those higher levels. Rigorous lessons incorporate elements of support in four ways: scaffolding within lessons, incorporating motivational elements, addressing strategic knowledge, and providing extra help.

Scaffolding Within Lessons

One of the most important aspects of supporting students to higher levels of rigor is incorporating additional scaffolding throughout the regular instruction. This can occur in a variety of ways, but it requires that teachers considering every step of their lesson, "What extra support might my students need?"

Sample Scaffolding Strategies

- Chunking Information
- Color-Coding Steps in a Project
- Writing standards as questions for students to answer
- Using visuals and graphic organizers, such as a math graphic organizer, for word problems
- Providing tools such as Interactive Reading Guides, Guide-o-Ramas

---

These and other ideas are included in *Classroom Instruction from A to Z* (2007), *Literacy from A to Z* (2008), and *Rigor is Not a Four-Letter Word* (2008).

Incorporating Motivational Elements

If you've read *Classroom Motivation from A to Z*, you know that Barbara believes all students are motivated, just not necessarily by the things we would like. Many of her students were not motivated by a desire to learn; rather, they were motivated by the approval of their friends, or the wish to earn some money, or something else in their lives. In her school, she had a basic system of positive and negative consequences, but it seemed to yield temporary results. She used praise and rewards in her classroom, but with less emphasis, learning that it was more important for students to be intrinsically motivated. The job of a teacher is to create an environment in which students are more likely to be motivated.

Students are more motivated when they value what they are doing and when they believe they have a chance for success. Those are the two keys:

value and success. Do students see value or the relevance in lessons? Do they believe they can be successful?

Student Motivation	
Creating Value	*Creating Success*
◆ use a variety of activities ◆ design "attractive" lessons ◆ provide some student choice ◆ help students understand why its important and/or useful ◆ be positive and have fun	◆ make assignments challenging but within the students ability to complete ◆ build on other successes ◆ provide encouragement ◆ learn about others who failed before they succeeded

Addressing Strategic Knowledge

Another important aspect of supporting students is to address strategic knowledge. We often focus on prior knowledge of students, especially related to the content of a lesson. However, it's easy to forget strategic knowledge, which is the knowledge instructional strategy we expect from students. For example, we often expect students to know how to listen, take notes, or use the textbook. In moving to more rigorous text for reading, however, a student may not know how to handle that text. There are two solutions to this issue. First, teachers can teach or review appropriate strategies with students. Second, they can provide tools, such as a guide-o-rama, which can teach or remind students of appropriate strategies.

Providing Extra Help

Finally, even with the strongest support during regular instructional time, there are students who need additional help. Although we will address how to build structures for extra help more specifically in Chapter Eleven; let's look at a couple of key points. First, extra help for students who are struggling should not be optional. Students who need the most help are least likely to ask for it. Often, they don't even realize they need help. Therefore, schools should offer optional opportunities, such as tutoring, but teachers should identify students who need more support and the school should provide that in a supportive, but required manner.

Extra help should also be offered during the school day, or some of your most at-risk students will not be able to access it. One school offered tutoring for every student after school. However, in analyzing their data, they discovered that students making poor grades were not staying for tutoring. With further research, it became evident these students did not have transportation home if they stayed for tutoring. Again, designing structures to provide help to students is addressed in detail in Chapter Eleven.

Things You Might Ask Your Teachers

- What ways do you demonstrate that students are not allowed not to learn?
- How do you customize support so that students learn?
- What strategies do you find most effective for encouraging student success?

Ensuring Students Demonstrate Learning at High Levels

Finally, in a rigorous classroom, *each student demonstrates learning at high levels.* You might think, "If teachers provide more challenging lessons that include extra support, won't this last part just happen?" Nothing "just happens." If we want students to show us they understand what they learned at a high level, we also need to provide opportunities to demonstrate they have truly mastered new content. Let's look at four ways to do so: increased student engagement, challenging and varied assessments, clear standards and rubrics, and multiple options to demonstrate understanding.

Characteristics of Demonstrating Learning at High Levels

- Increased Student Engagement
- Clear Standards and Rubrics
- Challenging Assessments
- Multiple Options to Demonstrate Understanding

Increased Student Engagement

You might think it is surprising that increased student engagement is an indicator of demonstration of learning. However, it is a critical aspect of rigor. For example, in many classrooms, the bulk of instruction consists of the teacher teaching to the entire class, perhaps in an interactive lecture or discussion format. The general practice during these lessons is that the teacher asks a question, and then he or she calls on a student to answer the question. Although this provides an opportunity for one student to demonstrate understanding, the remaining students are not allowed to do so. If, instead, the teacher allows all students to respond either through pair-share, thumbs up or down, writing an answer on small whiteboards and showing them, or responding on a handheld computer for a tally, then each student is allowed—indeed required—to demonstrate understanding.

Indicators of High Student Engagement	
Negative Indicators	*Positive Indicators*
♦ One student responds ♦ Two or three students discuss content ♦ Students are asked if they understand, with a simple yes or no and no probing.	♦ All students respond ♦ All students discuss content in small groups ♦ All students write a response in a journal or exit slip

Things You Might Ask Your Teachers

♦ What are some ways you make your lessons engaging to students?
♦ How do you monitor your students' engagement?
♦ Talk with me about how you make decisions about making your lessons engaging?

Clear Standards and Rubrics

A second factor with students demonstrating understanding is the need for them to understand exactly what that is. A particular issue for many students is not knowing what good looks like. Students are asked to complete an assignment, and then a teacher is disturbed when the quality of work does not match his or her expectations. This can lead to frustration for teachers and students. At times students simply don't know what to do, how to do it, or they think what they are doing is right. This happens more frequently when students are asked to do more rigorous work.

The solution to this is straightforward. Students need to have explicit standards for work. Then, they need a clear rubric or set of criteria that define "what good looks like." Additionally, it is helpful if students can see several models of quality work so they have a benchmark.

Challenging Assessments

Next, consider the assessments used with students. Are they challenging? What percentage of the assessments used during a grading period are tests vs. projects? How many include higher order thinking skills? How many demand open-ended responses? When we present this material in our workshops, we are often asked, are you saying we can't use a test? No. Testing is an appropriate part of assessment. But there are good tests and poor tests. One simple adjustment that can be made relates to true/false questions. Rather than having students label a series of statements as true or false, require them to take any false statement and rewrite it as a true statement. This one change is more rigorous and requires students to show they truly understand the content.

Multiple Options to Demonstrate Understanding

Teachers may choose to use a test to check for mastery of content, but there are alternatives that move beyond testing. Varying the types of assessments will produce quality, sometimes from unexpected sources. For example, Kendra Alston, a middle school instructional facilitator in North Carolina, shares a story from her own experience. Her high school social studies teacher gave a "show me what you know" exam. He said the format didn't matter, as long as you showed what you knew. Kendra completed in-depth research of the historical period of the 1920s and 1930s, far more than she would have completed for a standard test. She used the theatre and vaudeville circuit as her organizing theme, and came to class in character as Bessie Smith, a period singer. She described the time period through Bessie's eyes, earned an A, and today is still excited discussing the assessment.

Many teachers also use differentiated instruction and multiple intelligences to provide alternatives for students to demonstrate understanding. You can find a multiple examples in Barbara's other books for teachers: *Classroom Motivation from A to Z*, *Classroom Instruction from A to Z*, and *Literacy from A to Z*. The most important point is that you integrate knowledge of multiple intelligences to provide students' choices in assessments.

As a school leader, you will want to talk with your teachers about the different ways they ask students to demonstrate their learning.

Final Thoughts

We suspect that you find that you are already using some of the ideas and we know that every school community is unique. Throughout the book, we purposely included many different examples and encourage you to adapt them to fit your own setting. We believe that rigor does not necessarily mean throwing away everything you are doing. Rigor in many cases means adjusting what you do to increase your expectations and the learning of your students.

4

The BASE Planning Model

We believe that schools must routinely monitor their work and make improvements in response to changes in students, expectations, or other contextual issues.

We've been involved in many planning projects and have come to appreciate that schools are constantly improving. This continuous improvement process is described many ways but we've developed our BASE model to describe what we suggest you do. We chose BASE because everything you do to improve rigor must be built on a solid base, one that reflects research and best practice, builds support among teachers and families, and includes solid measures for success.

In Chapter One, we introduced our COMPASS model that includes seven key strategies you can use to improve rigor in your school. We like the compass as a metaphor because it shows the way and always points to "true north." Compasses are most effective when they sit on a BASE, one that provides a firm and steady foundation.

The four stages of the BASE model reflect a commitment to continuous improvement.

The model provides a way to organize the steps you will take to achieve your vision for a more rigorous school. It is circular in nature and assumes that to sustain improvements in rigor, you must study how you have done and that this study will naturally lead to identifying additional ways your school can be more rigorous.

BASE Planning Model

Step 4: Evaluate and Adjust

Step 1: Begin to Plan

Step 3: Sustain Success

Step 2: Act to Implement

Step 1: Beginning the Planning

We've identified some strategies that you can use to work with teachers, families, and communities to improve the rigor of your school. They are much like a set of tools. Not every tool works for every job. Some tasks require more than one tool. Most important is the ability to figure out which tool best fits the situation and will work most effectively.

Most importantly they recognize the importance of using an inclusive process that is focused on making your vision for a more rigorous school a reality.

Checklist of Planning Activities

_____ 1. Are critical stakeholders involved?

_____ 2. Is there an agreed upon mission/vision for a rigorous school?

_____ 3. Do we have the data and information about our current conditions?

_____ 4. Is there an agreed upon process for making decisions?

_____ 5. How will we share information with others?

Use an Inclusive Process

Involving all stakeholders builds greater commitment to change. That is particularly true when you're talking about increasing rigor. We've learned that when teachers get involved in discussing ways to improve rigor, they are more likely to change what they do.

Any plans to increase rigor also must include families and community as well as teachers and other school staff. They are integral partners in nurturing and sustaining a culture of rigor and supporting the school's efforts at home and in the greater community.

Be Clear About Group Operations

We believe strongly in a collaborative approach and have found that groups are most successful when they have a clear process to guide their deliberations.

First, we believe that use of an agreed upon set of norms about group operations and decision-making is critical. Garmston and Wellman (1999) suggest a set of seven norms of collaboration. Information about the norms, including a self-assessment that may be used by any group is available at http://www.adaptiveschools.com.

When Ron worked at Hadley Junior High School in Glen Ellyn, IL, he learned about the norms they used, their "Professional Behavior Norms."

Professional Behavior Norms

1. The learning that occurs today belongs to you, and it rests largely with you.
2. Enter into the discussion enthusiastically.
3. Give freely of your experience, but don't dominate the discussion.
4. Confine your discussion to the task assigned.
5. Say what you think . . . be honest.
6. Only one person should talk at a time. Avoid private conversations while someone else is talking.
7. Listen attentively to the presentation and discussion.
8. Be patient with other participants. Appreciate their point-of-view.

Identify a Process for Making Decisions

It is also important to be clear about how decisions will be made. It is much easier to talk about a decision-making process at the beginning rather than when a decision must be made. Consensus is always the goal but occasionally that doesn't work and groups need to be clear about how decisions will be made.

Deciding on a course of action can be a challenge and is frequently contentious, particularly if the decision is made by voting. Voting tends to create winners and losers. There are several other ways to make decisions. They include multi-voting, use of a consensogram, and the "Fist to Five." Chapter Six will share additional ideas about making decisions.

It is important to be clear about both the task of the group and the timeline for completing their work. A teacher in one of the schools where Ron worked said, "We've found we can talk anything to death. We talk and talk and nothing gets decided or changed. Eventually the issue just goes away." Sadly, that characterizes the work in many schools. Provide a clear description of the task for the group and the date by which they should complete their work.

Provide a Common Base of Information

Everyone involved in the work to increase rigor should have access to the same data and have an opportunity to look at the same print and electronic resources. Often, families, students, and community members feel as though teachers and principals have "privileged" information. Occasionally even some teachers don't have the same information, especially when someone shares specific content area knowledge.

Establish a norm that no one can talk about the "research" without providing everyone access to the research. ACT, SREB, and the College Board are great sources of research. Be sure that opinions or experience are accurately labeled, not used as conclusive evidence.

One school outside of Chicago where Ron worked provided everyone involved in the discussion with a common set of readings. They included data about community demographics, information on career trends, resources on successful instructional practices, and future trends. These readings became the basis for many of the discussions about increasing rigor in the school.

Anchor Your Plan in a Shared Vision

Any discussion about improving rigor must be based on a shared vision. A clear and compelling vision and mission reflects the collective commitment of a school community and serves as one way to link programs and practices to a common goal.

If your school's mission statement hasn't been updated in several years, it may be time to review it and make necessary changes.

The staff at one southeastern Michigan high school recognized that their students could no longer rely on getting high-paying jobs in the automobile industry upon graduation. This change along with the general economic malaise led the principal to propose a re-examination of the school's mission. While the final statement was quite similar to the previous statement, the process led to a collective recommitment to improving the school's program focused on assuring that every graduate could meet more rigorous graduation requirements.

Vision is one of the most effective tools for personal and group motivation. Having a vision, then revisiting it regularly, helps you and your faculty focus on what is important and assists in balancing competing demands for your time and energy. Chapter Six provides a tool you can use to revise your school's mission.

Commit to the Use of Data

Groups that use member's opinions as the primary source of data almost always find themselves unable to make progress. We've found that the most productive groups are comfortable gathering and analyzing data independent of individuals' experience or opinion.

It is important to gather data about student learning. Put together a portfolio of materials that reflects the academic expectations of students, the quality of their work, and the success on agreed upon measures of academic success.

It may also be useful to conduct a self-assessment of your school's current efforts to increase rigor. Andrew Nelson, Associate Principal at Oregon High School in Oregon, IL, used Barbara's rubric from *Rigor is Not a Four-Letter Word* and turned it into a short survey. The staff completed the survey and the results were used to guide their further work to increase rigor. Here is a short section of their survey.

School Academic Climate Survey

1. Which of the following statements best applies to you in your expectations for your students?
   a) I am still working to understand what it means that all students can learn at high levels.
   b) I believe that all students can learn at high levels and I sometimes act on those beliefs with some of my students.

---

  c) I believe that all students can learn at high levels and I consistently act on those beliefs with all of my students.
2. Which of the following statements best applies to you in helping your students achieve at higher academic levels?
  a) I have an occasional general support system. I also provide optional extra help.
  b) I have a customized support system for each of my students that I sometimes use to help ensure their success. I also provide optional extra help.
  c) I have a customized support system for each of my students that I use consistently that encourages my students to be independent learners. Students are required to receive extra help if they need it.

From: Oregon High School, Oregon, IL

Another way to provide data is to ask an external observer to visit your school and provide feedback on ways to increase rigor. Both of us make these visits and provide our recommendations for improvement.

When District 203 in Naperville, IL began to talk about ways to improve rigor in their middle school program they invited Ron to visit and spend time in each of the schools. He met with several small groups of teachers, students, and parents, conducted classroom walkthroughs, and watched the general pattern of activity throughout the schools. He provided some immediate feedback to the staff at each school and, after the visit, provided a much more detailed set of recommendations to the district. These recommendations became the base for further planning.

Suggestions for Collecting Additional Data

- ◆ Conduct a self-assessment
- ◆ Arrange for an external review by someone knowledgeable about rigor
- ◆ Organize a shadow study of students (see Chapter Seven)
- ◆ Hold a focus group discussion with students, parents, or teachers

---

Step 2: Act to Implement the Plan

As complex as planning can be, implementing and sustaining those changes can be even more of a challenge. It is the implementation that forces people to face the reality that things "may be different." The reality of implementation can provoke a range of feelings including regret over abandoning familiar practices, exhilaration at the prospect of new ideas, or of being overwhelmed by the complexity of doing something new.

Checklist of Planning Activities

_____	1. Have you created a culture of collegiality?
_____	2. Do you have a process for gathering initial data about implementation and monitoring the implementation?
_____	3. Do you have a process to gather initial data about implementation?
_____	4. What opportunities have you planned for teachers to talk about and share their successes and challenges?
_____	5. Is there an agreed upon process for making decisions?
_____	6. How will we share information with others?

There are several strategies and tools that you may want to consider as you work with your school community to implement plans to increase rigor.

Have a Plan for Monitoring the Implementation

Few changes go perfectly when implemented. Even with ample time to plan, extensive professional development, and sufficient resources, it is likely that some issues will emerge that require attention.

When this occurs it is important to maintain a focus on improvement and not become overly defensive. We've found the following strategies to be very helpful.

Look at the Data Gather and review any relevant data. It may be helpful to talk with groups of teachers about their experience. Look for patterns in their comments. Chapter Seven provides examples of ways to collect data and then use data to guide decisions about improving rigor.

Provide Time to Reflect on and Discuss the Issues Provide an opportunity for groups or individuals to share their concerns and discuss the implications. Some individuals may want to talk privately but we've found that it is helpful to have a process for structured feedback about an innovation.

There are several ways to focus this feedback but Ron has used two successfully with schools—a Plus/Delta process and the Quality Quadrant process. Both recognize that there are both positive things about any implementation as well as ways to get better.

Leadership in Action

Mark Ravlin, the Executive Director for Improvement, in Adrian, MI, asked district planning committees to use the Plus/Delta process, a continuous improvement tool that allows a group to identify positive things about an activity as well as opportunities for improvement. Pluses identify things that are working and things that can be built upon. Deltas are things that can be improved or changed so that the plan could be more effective. They are best when action oriented and begin with a verb. Both should be reviewed and acted upon as soon as possible but action does not mean agreeing with each suggestion.

+	Δ

At Hadley Junior High in Glen Ellyn, IL, the planning committee used a "Quality Quadrants" tool to gather feedback from staff about suggested school improvement activities. Each teacher made comments in each of the categories and the school improvement team used the comments to guide their work.

Topic:	
Concerns	Kudos
Suggestions for Improvement	Questions

Don't Rush to Judgment Be cautious about rushing to change things too quickly. It is very common for an implementation slump to occur. By that we mean that during the first few months of implementation many teachers may still be learning how to fully implement the innovation. Don't rush to change things before you have sufficient data about the need.

When Ron was working in Tempe, AZ one of the middle schools reorganized its instructional teams. By early October of the first year many teachers were concerned that the changes weren't working for eighth graders. After talking with students it became clear that the issue was that the eighth graders weren't committed to a new model for one year. Choosing to persevere, the staff found that there were no implementation issues the second year. The new instructional model was accepted as "just the way we do things here."

Make Appropriate Adjustments On the other hand, you should never continue to implement a strategy that clearly is not working. If the data show that there is a need to re-think part of your plan you should do so. Often, you may learn that you may need additional professional development or more time for planning. Either way, stay focused on assuring that the implementation is successful and positively benefits students.

Nurture a Collegial Culture

Schools where the leader has created a collegial culture have a better chance of success. Roland Barth, one of the nation's leading school improvement experts, suggests that:

> A precondition for doing anything to strengthen our practice and improve a school is the existence of a collegial culture in which professionals talk about practice, share their craft knowledge, and observe and root for the success of one another. Without these in place, no meaningful improvement—is possible. (Barth, 2006)

The culture of your school is pivotal to your success. Chapter Five will discuss culture and ways you can create a culture that supports improved rigor for every student. Here are some questions you may want to consider as you begin to act on your plan.

COMPASS Tool	Leadership Strategies
Culture	♦ How do you create a sense of urgency about the need to improve rigor? ♦ How do you nurture and support a culture of collaboration focused on rigor? ♦ What do you do to develop a collegial relationship with teachers and staff?
Ownership and Shared Vision	♦ How do you engage teachers, staff, and families in developing a shared vision for rigor in your school? ♦ What strategies do you use to build ownership and commitment to this vision? ♦ What are the ways you've found helpful to involve stakeholders in developing a vision of a more rigorous school?
Managing Data	♦ What types of data do you and your staff gather and use to guide your efforts to become a more rigorous school? ♦ What are the agreed upon measures of success for monitoring your progress? ♦ How do you use data to measure progress?

Professional Development	◆ What professional development is needed to support your school's vision of improved rigor? ◆ What resources are available to guide selection of professional development? ◆ How does professional development link to the implementation of more rigorous instruction?
Advocacy	◆ What ways do you share your personal vision of a rigorous school with teachers and other staff as well as parents and the school community? ◆ How will you and others work with parents and the larger school community to create a culture of rigor? ◆ What strategy will you use to create support for rigor among school stakeholders?
Structure	◆ What resources are needed to ensure success of your efforts to improve rigor? ◆ How do you use time, personnel, and financial resources to support your school's vision of improved rigor? ◆ How will we support students, families, and the community as you become a more rigorous school?
Shared Accountability	◆ How do you build a sense of mutual responsibility and accountability for rigor? ◆ What strategies will you use to help families support increased rigor? ◆ How do we build a community commitment to our vision of a more rigorous school?

Remove Barriers to Action

How you perceive roadblocks determines your response. Rather than seeing roadblocks as barriers, view them as opportunities. Richard Benjamin, former superintendent in Nashville and suburban Atlanta, suggested that our critics are really our best friends because they force us to be clearer about our beliefs, to look more closely at our plans, and further consider the implications of our thinking.

That attitude can help a leader deal with what may appear to be insurmountable roadblocks; things that slow down or stop implementation of your plan to improve rigor

We've identified several strategies that leaders can use to find a way around the roadblocks that emerge when you work to increase the rigor of your instructional program.

Constructively Deal with Conflict

Many school improvement plans never get implemented because either the leaders or teachers seek to avoid the conflict associated with the change. As we discussed earlier, not everyone will be supportive of change. Some will actively resist. Many will simply disengage and hope the change goes away.

There is no guarantee that implementing your plan to improve rigor will be free of all conflict. There are, however, some things you can do to minimize and deal constructively with conflict. You might want to try the following.

Strategies for Dealing with Conflict

◆ Use data and descriptions to talk about issues, not value judgments or personal interpretations

◆ Focus on the present, not what was or might have been

◆ Own your own ideas and feelings; use "I" as much as possible when conveying your ideas

◆ Explain, do not defend

◆ Be attentive to non-verbal clues and messages

◆ Assume the motives of others are "honorable"

◆ Avoid the use of superlatives or absolutes like most, best, always, or never

◆ Agree when those of another viewpoint are right

◆ Use active listening skills

We've found that one of the most useful strategies for dealing with conflict is to build positive relationships with people. When conflict arises you can drawn on your reservoir of good will to help get past the difference of opinion.

Establish Accountability for Results

Accountability is critical. It should not be punitive or heavy-handed but it must be clearly defined and steadfastly implemented. Teachers and other staff must recognize their accountability for implementing the plan to improve rigor, for collecting and using data to guide implementation, and for engaging in collegial conversations about their work.

As school leaders we learned that it is important to continue to support staff during implementation. Few things work exactly as planned. It is necessary to provide support and encouragement and maintain a focus on the goal.

Continue to invest in professional development. Often important questions emerge only once an innovation has begun. Too often, professional development occurs prior to implementation. We've found that it is helpful to create structures that allow staff to share their experience with change and support one another during implementation.

Leadership in Action

Nancy York, principal of Fox Technical High School in San Antonio, organized a series of Café Conversations for her teachers. Each meeting was designed to focus on a single experience with increasing expectations for quality work among ninth graders. The sessions provided an opportunity for teachers to share their successes, suggest other strategies for improvement, and support trying new practices. She reported that these "teacher-to-teacher" conversations were invaluable in helping her teachers change their practices.

The conversations were held in a room that looked like an actual café. Round tables with tablecloths and a small vase of flowers contributed to the atmosphere. Snacks and beverages were available.

The café was open all day and teachers were asked to stop in during their planning time and contribute to the conversation. Chart paper was used to record ideas. By the end of the each day, this collective knowledge was available to guide further improvement.

The focus at this school was not on barriers to implementation but on identifying successes and continuing to support one another as they worked to improve the rigor for every ninth grader.

The importance of shared accountability will be discussed further in Chapter Ten.

Step 3: Sustain Success

We've found that when your work is guided by a shared vision for a rigorous school and rigorous classrooms and where teachers and other school staff are actively involved in planning and implementation that change is more likely to be sustained. When change is the result of the personal vision of one or two people, the change is more likely to be abandoned as soon as its advocates leave.

It is critical, therefore, that leaders create a culture that supports innovation and builds capacity for long-term changes in their school's program.

The third step of our planning model focuses on sustaining success. Earlier we discussed ways to monitor the implementation. We suggest you continue those activities. In addition, we encourage you to provide continued support for the implementation and begin to build internal capacity with teacher leaders so that the commitment to increased rigor is nurtured and sustained.

Checklist of Planning Activities

_____ 1. Do you have a plan for monitoring the success of your plan, identifying next steps, and suggesting appropriate changes?

_____ 2. Is there time for teachers to work with colleagues to share successes and participate in professional development?

_____ 3. What steps will you take to create a culture that will sustain the improvements?

_____ 4. How will you gather data and use that data to guide decisions?

_____ 5. What is your plan for celebrating successes?

Continue to Provide Support for Success

You need to build a structure that supports success. Too often support declines after the initial flurry of activity. Continue to provide professional development for teachers, collaborative time for teachers to work with one another, and supplies and materials needed to make the project succeed. That means organizing to monitor the implementation and make decisions about any modifications. It also means gathering and sharing information with stakeholders and providing time for collaboration and collegial conversation.

Monitor the Implementation If you have not already done so it is important to organize a group to monitor the continued implementation of your plan. The group should represent all of the important groups in your school, develop the skills for collaborative work, and be committed to using data to guide decisions about further program implementation.

Identify Time for Collaboration It is important that teachers have time to talk with colleagues about their professional work. We've found that this collaborative time is one of the catalysts for nurturing and sustaining change.

Teachers value the opportunity to meet with grade or content peers to discuss successes, diagnose ways to improve, and develop a repertoire of strategies that they can use in their own classrooms.

Here some of the ways we've found to provide collaborative time. These and other ideas will be discussed in Chapter Eleven.

Ways to Provide Collaborative Time

- Common content or grade level planning
- Parallel scheduling
- Adjusting the start and end of the day
- Use of faculty meetings
- Professional development days

Create a Culture of Continuous Improvement

Can real change occur in your school or classroom if the climate and culture doesn't change? No! Real change that will be sustained over time requires a significant change in the culture of your school (see Chapter Five), in people's attitudes (see Chapter Ten) and in structures and practices (see Chapter Eleven).

The most successful schools are places where there is a collective commitment to continuous improvement. Teachers and administrators recognize the need to regularly monitor what they are doing and make adjustments to assure the success of every student.

Regularly recognizing and celebrating positive examples of rigor will reinforce the commitment to a rigorous school and classrooms. Creating structures to monitor the implementation of your plans and make appropriate adjustments signals your comfort with change. Most of all, teachers, parents, and students look to the leader for assurance that your plans are thoughtful, carefully implemented, and routinely monitored.

Use Data to Study the Results

There is often a tendency to make decisions about programs based on informal data such as people's feelings or personal experiences. While interesting, we've found that it is more useful to agree upon indicators that will be used to monitor your success.

Once you have agreed on measures of improved rigor you must routinely gather the data and use it to guide decisions that sustain implementation.

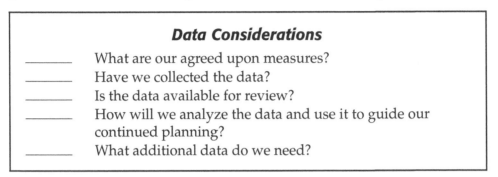

Data is most useful when it includes multiple measures—different types of data and when it is longitudinal—covers more than a single year.

Even more important than gathering data is to use it to help inform decisions. Work with others to identify patterns or trends. For example, look for trends in student test scores or patterns across students and family responses.

It is always helpful to have more than a single person look at the data. A more thoughtful analysis of data occurs when multiple perspectives and points-of-view are present in the discussion.

One school Ron worked with in Texas had an informal set of norms for using data.

Informal Norms
◆ Always use more than one type of data when making decisions
◆ Support every suggestion with data, not opinions
◆ Look for patterns across data sources
◆ Rely most on data from more than one year

Identify Successes and Celebrate

Effective schools celebrate small wins frequently. Have you every heard the statement, "success breeds success?" It's true. Celebrating small gains on a regular basis can motivate teachers and students. Over time, small, steady gains add up to real growth.

Create a culture that celebrates authentic success. Keep data on school and classroom efforts, monitor their impact, and celebrate on a regular basis.

Other Ways to Sustain Success

First, help everyone involved see the value of your efforts to improve rigor by providing clear, compelling rationale. Use data that are clear, meaningful, and linked to student success. Indicate how people can get involved in efforts to sustain the project.

Second, develop a mechanism for gathering and sharing information with teachers and other stakeholders. For example, develop a plan for talking with teachers about how they are succeeding in making their classroom more rigorous. Ask parents about the experience of their children as your school becomes more rigorous.

Step 4: Evaluate and Adjust

The very best schools constantly monitor their performance and identify ways to continue to make improvements. The final stage of our BASE planning model is to "Evaluate and Adjust." As we said, the planning process is circular. The decisions you make during this stage will naturally lead you to continue planning to become even more rigorous.

As with the other steps there are several important considerations. Because we discussed them earlier we will not repeat them, but here are some of the most important activities for evaluating and adjusting your plan.

Checklist of Planning Activities

1. Do you have a process to evaluate the success of your plan and identify next steps?
2. Have you gathered the data to make informed decisions about your progress?
3. What plans are developed for sharing your plans with teachers, families, and community?

Ensure Positive Dynamics Among School Personnel

It is important that you nurture and sustain a collaborative culture, one that embraces open, honest conversation about improving rigor. You may discover some part of the plan needs additional attention or that additional professional development will be helpful.

That's normal. You need to resist the tendency to point fingers, to blame other people, or factors outside of your school. We don't ever believe that is helpful. The power to monitor implementation and adjust plans lies within the school with teachers and administrators.

We've worked with hundreds of schools in every region of the United States and identified behaviors that can be harmful to your success. Similarly, we've identified behaviors that can support your culture of collaboration and your work to make your school more rigorous.

Inhibitors	*Facilitators*
People are reluctant to share data about things that aren't working.	People are comfortable sharing data about what doesn't work. They are not penalized for doing so.

People use opinions, rather than data, to support their positions.	People support their suggestions with data, facts, and solid logic.
People agree to a decision, yet do little to support its success.	People support mutually agreed upon decisions and work to make the decision succeed.
People seek personal credit for success.	People credit others for success.
People disagree to improve their own interests rather than to find the best answer.	People are comfortable disagreeing and focused on finding the best response to the current issue.
People find blame, seeking culprits, rather than identifying causes.	People analyze experiences to identify ways to improve.
People blame people or conditions outside of the school for lack of success.	People accept full responsibility for successes as well as failures.
The leader avoids critical input and does not ask questions to clarify thinking.	The leader asks lots of questions, challenges thinking, and values discussion and critical insight into issues.

Adapted from: Collins (2009)

Data, Data, Data

Data is really important. Chapter Seven will provide a more thorough discussion about how to use data to guide your decisions. But we want to be clear, that decisions about evaluating and adjusting your plans must use data about student learning, preferably types of data that were identified when you began planning to improve rigor in your school.

Be clear about norms you will use to talk about the data. Avoid reliance on personal opinion or "experience." But be comfortable challenging the data, asking probing questions, and identifying additional data that you may want to collect.

You may also want to invite an external expert to visit your school to conduct an assessment of your efforts to improve rigor. Here is an example of recommendations that Barbara provided to Dutch Form Middle School in Irmo, SC after such a visit. The recommendations only reflect general patterns of behavior in the school and should never be used as part of a school or individual teacher evaluation.

Recommendations for Increasing Rigor

These recommendations are based on 43 individual classroom walkthroughs and a review of assessments provided by teachers. Please note the information relates to overall patterns in the school and does not focus on individual subjects and teachers.

Student Engagement in Learning

There are varying levels of student engagement. While some of this might be attributed to the specific tasks of the lesson, this is an area in which you can build on strengths to maximize learning. Generally, whole group activities are less engaging than small group activities and offer more opportunities for students to "tune out." This is closely linked to the questioning. Truly rigorous expectations include the expectation that each student will answer, and as such, opportunities are given for all students to answer, rather than simply listening to one another answer.

Recommendations:
Build on current strengths, such as having students work together to solve problems or complete tasks. Continuing those activities that require all students to participate, whether through the use of technology, dry erase boards, or simple hand movements will send a message that all students are expected to learn, not simply those with raised hands. Insist on all students participating in instruction, utilizing all appropriate class time. There are classrooms in which the level of engagement is very high; build on that for consistency.

Share What You Are Doing

It is important to have a plan for sharing your work with teachers, families, and community. Chapter Nine shares several specific strategies that you might use to share information and advocate for your vision of a more rigorous school.

A collective commitment to improved rigor is anchored in a shared vision and confidence that the plan is collaboratively developed. Your evaluation plans should strengthen this confidence through wide dissemination of both the plan and the findings.

Sharing Results

- Share the results with stakeholder groups
- Acknowledge both strengths and weaknesses
- Disseminate information widely
- Provide time for ample discussion of the results
- Use data to guide continued planning

Leadership in Action

When Hadley Junior High in Glen Ellyn, IL began a project to change the curriculum and instructional practices, the planning team developed a plan for routinely communicating with teachers and other staff and with parents.

At the end of every planning meeting a set of "talking points" were agreed to by those present. They were then shared with every teacher via e-mail. The talking points and information about every planning meeting were posted in a visible location in the main school hallway.

Months before the school began to implement the changes they held monthly "open forums" where teachers and staff could meet with members of the planning team to learn about the project and to ask questions about implementation. The meetings alternated between before school and after school.

The planning team also held a series of "Community Forums" for parents and other community members. Each forum provided an opportunity to learn about some aspect of the program changes. They also included an opportunity for parents to ask specific, targeted questions about the rationale and impact of the changes.

Final Thoughts

Because schools are under increasing pressure to improve the educational experience of students there is a tendency to want immediate results from any innovation. This leads many schools to weave from one improvement strategy to another without clear vision and purpose, and without a clear sense of when they will be successful.

Thoughtful planning and careful implementation are important. But no step is more important than taking the time to nurture and support your efforts to improve rigor. It is essential to monitor the implementation, gather and use data about your success, and find ways to support the teachers and other staff who work daily with your students.

5

Culture

Have you ever felt like you were swimming against the current? That's exactly the feeling expressed by an assistant principal during a recent conversation.

> We've been focusing on rigor for the last two years. We paid a lot of money for a consulting group to help us increase rigor in our schools. In all the workshops, they talked about rigor and how important it is to change what we do in our classrooms. Some of the speakers could have been better, but they weren't bad. Yet here we are, two years later, and nothing has changed. I'm tired of talking about rigor. I'm ready to do something about it!

Unfortunately, that is all too common. We know something needs to change; we analyze our data, build a plan, and provide professional development, yet the changes are minimal. That's because we often fail to take into account the culture of the school.

Culture reflects the complex set of values, traditions, and patterns of behavior that are present in a school. Unlike school climate, the culture is indicative of the deeply embedded beliefs about schooling and reveals itself in "the unwritten rules and assumptions, the combination of rituals and traditions, the array of symbols and artifacts, the special language and phrasing that staff and students use, the expectations for change and learning" (Peterson & Deal, 2002).

The culture of a school is a powerful tool that leaders can use to shape the operation of their school and the behavior of those who work there (Williamson & Johnston, 2005). As schools face pressure to change, the introduction of reforms introduces uncertainty and unpredictability into the lives of people working in schools. Understanding culture, how it works, and how it can be shaped is an important tool for improving the rigor in a school's educational program.

The concept of school culture emerged from the work of Deal and Kennedy (1982), Deal and Peterson (1990), and Schein (1985). Two key ideas capture the idea. First, a school's culture reflects the informal, often unspoken, rules about how people behave. Second, a positive school culture can "enable people to feel better about what they do" (Deal & Kennedy, 1982, p. 16).

Schein (1985) identified several tools that leaders can use to embed and reinforce new norms in their organization. They include their response to critical events; their modeling, teaching, and coaching of other personnel; the criteria used to reward and recognize staff; and most importantly, what the leader pays attention to and measures.

Ways Leaders Can Impact Their School's Culture

♦ What leaders pay attention to, measure, and control becomes important;
♦ The leader's reactions to critical incidents and events;
♦ Role modeling, teaching, and coaching by leaders;
♦ The criteria for allocation of rewards and status in the school; and
♦ Criteria used for recruitment, selection, and promotion.

Adapted from: Schein (1985)

What does a rigorous culture look like?

In Chapter Three, we provided concrete examples of what rigor looks like in a school, broken down by expectations, support, and demonstration of student learning. A school with a rigorous culture incorporates rigor in all of those areas. For example, if your school offers rigorous curriculum, but the majority of the instruction is rote-memorization based, disengaging, and unmotivating to students, and does not offer scaffolding and support within and outside of class, then the overall culture of the school is not rigorous. The sample questions below will help you assess your culture, based on the specific categories from Chapter Three. Although they are yes/no questions, you should consider the evidence you have to support your answer.

Sample Questions to Assess Rigor in School Culture	
Expectations of Student Learning	
Challenging Curriculum	Is our curriculum challenging for all learners?
High Level Instruction	Do we consistently provide high levels of instruction for all learners?
Adult Behaviors	Do our behaviors, as adults, encourage students to rise to new levels of learning?
Support for Student Learning	
Scaffolding	Do we consistently provide appropriate scaffolding within lessons on an ongoing basis?
Incorporating Motivation	Do we consistently incorporate motivational elements into lessons?
Addressing Strategic Knowledge	Do we intentionally teach and reinforce strategic knowledge, in addition to content knowledge?
Providing Extra Help	Do we provide mandatory opportunities for extra help for those who need additional support, as well as optional times for any student who desired it?
Demonstration of Student Learning	
Increased Student Engagement	Do we engage students at high levels consistently throughout lessons?

Sample Questions to Assess Rigor in School Culture (continued)	
Clear Standards and Rubrics	Do we provide clear standards and rubrics so students understand the expectations we have?
Challenging Assessments	Are our assessments challenging to student? Do we define challenging by criteria other than grades or the number of students who fail a test?
Multiple Options to Demonstrate Learning	Do we provide multiple options for students to demonstrate their understanding of content? Do we move beyond standardized testing for this?

What is the role of the leader?

We spoke with one new principal who commented, "The culture in this school is just too traditional. I'm the new person, and there's really nothing I can do to change it." We disagree. Of course, it will take time and patience, but your role as a leader is critical. A principal we worked with concurs, saying, "The school leader is most influential in creating and maintaining a rigorous culture. Without leadership, expectations will wane and outcomes will be mixed at best.

What are the symbolic aspects of a rigorous culture?

Culture reflects the unspoken norms about school operations, and is transmitted from generation to generation, often by the influential staff that others recognize as informal leaders and opinion leaders. Bolman and Deal (2003) provide a model for understanding the things that contribute to culture. It is based on the idea that every organization has a culture that reflects underlying values, which are patterns of shared basic assumptions. These assumptions are often passed from generation to generation, taught to new members of the culture, whether teachers, students, or parents, as the "way we do things around here" (Bower, 1996).

Over time every school develops its own personality. This is shaped by the people who work in the school, the community the school serves, the students who attend the school and the way these groups respond to the successes, tragedies, and daily events at the school. Culture is a powerful set of rituals, traditions, and practices that reflect the values of a school. For example, there is often a tension between the importance of athletics and academics. If a community chose to spend more on an athletic facility than on school renovations, it says something about values. Or if a school adopted a stance that every child will read by the end of the second grade, it says something about values.

You can impact your school's culture by using these symbols to promote institutional values and the school's core mission. Most importantly, if you understand the power of these symbols, you can use them to telegraph messages about "what is important."

Organizational Symbols that Reflect Culture

1. Rituals and Ceremonies—provide structure to our daily life and to the routine of a school. Rituals occur rather routinely while ceremonies are grander, less frequent events (graduation). Both rituals and ceremonies reflect values in their structure, their priority, and carry meaning about what is valued and what is important.

2. Heroes and Heroines—those people who are looked up to as reflecting the organization's values; people who are examples of living the values.

3. Stories and Tales—those recollections of events that are told and retold and play a powerful role in sharing examples of organizational values. Stories often contain a moral and are inevitably engaging.

4. Rewards and Reinforcements—They reflect those things that are valued and therefore rewarded. Is it creativity in the classroom or compliance with established patterns? Is it waiving a rule so that a student may be successful or adhering to established policy?

Successful school leaders recognize the power of culture to shape their school. They develop the capacity to deploy the tools in ways that reinforce the importance of rigor in their school's program.

You might want to make a quick assessment of your school's culture. If so, here are some things you might do to assess the culture of your school.

After you gather some of these data, identify any patterns you may find. What do they say about the culture in your school? How might you use the symbols of culture to improve the rigor of your school?

Rituals and Ceremonies

How can rituals or ceremonies promote rigor? There are a variety of ways. For example, in addition to celebrating top grades, also celebrate progress toward higher levels of achievement. In addition to an honor roll, publish a "Principal's Progress" list, which recognizes any student who has made progress over a certain period of time.

Principal's Progress Sample Items

♦ Students who increased grades or grade point averages
♦ Students who moved from a "not yet" to a minimum grade
♦ Students who revised work during an extra help session
♦ Students who support the academic progress of other students

One Michigan middle school starts every year with an opening day celebration. Students march to the athletic field carrying banners with their team name. Students who made exceptional academic progress the prior year are recognized and incoming students are introduced to the school's motto—"Excellence, Excellence, Excellence." Following the ceremony every team meets to set academic goals for the year and to talk about how exceptional student performance will be recognized.

Assess Your School...

♦ What regular routines tell you how rigorous the instruction is in your school?

♦ Is there a set of routines and rituals that clearly communicate your values about rigor? Do they work?

♦ Are there special ceremonies or events at your school that demonstrate a commitment to the success of every student?

♦ Do you use the recruitment and hiring of new teachers as a way to communicate values and shape culture?

A principal in Connecticut talked with Ron about how she makes sure that the hiring of new teachers conveys the school's commitment to a rigorous academic experience for students. "I've developed a set of questions that I ask of every candidate. If they're listening carefully, they will understand that this school values the success of every student and expects every student to succeed in a rigorous and challenging environment." The response from candidates provides this principal with clues about whether the candidates share the vision.

Heroes and Heroines

Who are the heroes and heroines in your efforts to increase rigor in your school? Which teacher is considered the most rigorous by parents, but is also the most respected?

At Mill Creek Middle School, an old rowboat found when the school was constructed hangs in the office. An oar found with the boat has become an important way to recognize staff members for their exceptional commitment to the success of students. Principal Evelyn Shirk started the process to "encourage the staff to never, ever accept less than student success."

Every month the oar is given to one teacher who "goes over and above" in their work with students. The principal dresses up as an old boatsman and interrupts one of the classes of the person being recognized. After a brief ceremony the oar remains in the teacher's classroom as a very visible recognition of their commitment to student success.

In suburban Seattle an elementary school principal uses every opportunity to celebrate teachers who take risks that contribute to student success. A bulletin board near the school lobby was used to recognize "Explorer's Heroes." It included a picture and description of teachers, staff, or students who reflected the school's academic mission and commitment to "students will not fail."

As with any recognition program it was important to only recognize people who had made authentic contributions. For example, one teacher changed how she grouped students for instruction even when other teachers at her grade level resisted the change.

Stories and Tales

What are the important stories that are told to newcomers? Are they stories about the support teachers feel when they demand high standards from their students? Are new students told that learning is not optional, that everyone in the school believes it is his or her responsibility to help each student learn? Do you hear turnaround stories about students who have overcome difficulties to learn at high levels?

The principal of a school in suburban Denver encouraged his teachers to "snitch" on other teachers who had some special success with students. Her goal was to find teachers who represented her school's commitment to a rigorous academic program complemented by high support. The principal delighted in sharing these stories with parents, with other district personnel, and with school staff. The goal was to create a culture of success and celebration of that success.

Similarly, a high school principal in suburban Tucson talked with Ron about how she worked with her staff to re-design their advisory program.

Working with the school improvement team a decision was made to provide increased academic support for students during this daily activity. The principal created a support and testing center where students could re-take tests that they previously failed. One veteran teacher took the lead on the project and used her personal credibility to advocate for this "new" approach. The principal revels in telling the story of this teacher and how she put "her personal reputation on the line to make a difference in the lives of our students." It is a powerful story.

Assess Your School . . .

♦ How do you communicate verbally and through your actions your commitment to the success of every student? To increasing the rigor of your school's program?

♦ What are the stories you tell about your school, its students, and staff? What stories do you encourage others to tell?

♦ What messages do you communicate in your daily actions, classroom visits, and other interactions with members of your school community?

♦ How do you nurture the storytellers on your staff? Do their stories reflect your school's values and mission?

Reward System

What is the reward system—both formal and informal? Are teachers rewarded for insisting that students complete their work at an acceptable level? Are students rewarded for progress in addition to high scores? In one school we worked with, each teacher had a bulletin board called "Soaring to Success." Students chose what would be posted, following a simple criterion: "Where are you making progress and what are you proud of?" Postings ranged from drafts of writing to a reworking of a complicated math problem.

It's also important to reward teachers who are leading or supporting increased levels of rigor. One way to do that is to keep a pad of "Recognizing Rigor" certificates, which you can use to acknowledge a teacher's work when conducting learning walks.

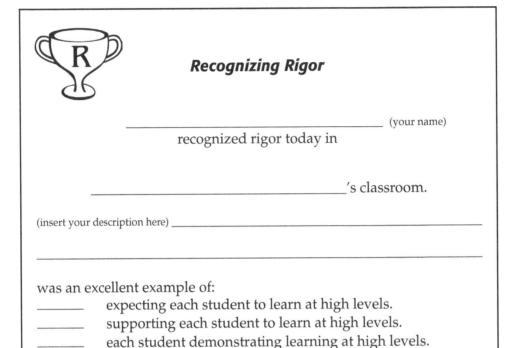

Recognizing Rigor

_____ (your name)

recognized rigor today in

_____'s classroom.

(insert your description here) _____

_____

was an excellent example of:

_____   expecting each student to learn at high levels.

_____   supporting each student to learn at high levels.

_____   each student demonstrating learning at high levels.

_____   creating an environment that supports rigor.

Thank you!

Teacher leadership will be discussed in Chapter Twelve: Challenges and Opportunities, but for now, we'd recommend you encourage teachers to also use the certificates. Give each teacher a handful and keep some near teacher mailboxes in your mailroom. As you model the use of the awards, promote the idea that everyone can and should recognize efforts toward increasing rigor.

Another way to build on this idea is "Name it, claim it, and explain it." As you see an example of rigorous work in a classroom, take a digital picture of what is happening. Begin each of your faculty meetings with a Power-Point slide of what you saw. The first item on your agenda is always a celebration of something positive related to rigor. Ask your faculty, "I saw something great related to rigor this week. It's up here on the screen. If it belongs to you, stand up and name what you did, claim it as yours, and explain what you were doing."

Regularly recognizing and celebrating positive examples of rigor will reinforce the commitment to a rigorous school and classrooms.

Summary of Symbolic Elements

A school's culture is reflected in the things that occur every day at the school. These "artifacts" reflect the school's espoused values and the basic underlying assumptions about schools and student learning.

Successful school leaders are skilled at diagnosing and monitoring their school's culture and using the factors discussed earlier to support their school's vision of a rigorous academic experience for students.

Cultural Factors	Examples
Rituals and Ceremonies	• Focus of school assemblies and other ceremonies • Daily announcements or daily bulletins
Heroes and Heroines	• Informal teacher leaders • Teachers admired by others for their work with students
Stories and Tales	• Stories shared with parents and other members of the school community • Examples told to new teachers
Reward System	• Formal and informal recognition systems • Use of budget for instructional materials and professional development

What are the structures that support a rigorous culture?

Another way to impact the culture of a school is through the structural elements. Without organizational structures to support change, it is like building castles in the air . . . you still need a ladder to get there.

An essential part of any change is building the capacity to support the change. Even the best ideas will fail at the first challenge if there is not a structural base for support. We've found that working with teachers and parents to both plan and monitor the implementation of new things is important. Assure that you have a system in place to "monitor and adjust" as needed. Chapter Four described in more detail how to sustain a more rigorous school program.

We recently saw this in a visit to a teacher's classroom. After attending one of Barbara's workshops, she decided to implement a "not yet" grading policy in her classroom. However, her efforts were quickly derailed, because she did not have a system for providing time and extra help for students who needed to rework an assignment. She offered an after-school tutoring session every Wednesday, but her students were reluctant to attend. After a conversation with the assistant principal and curriculum coach, they agreed to provide a "study session" during lunch for those students who needed to revise their work. The support and structured options provided by the school leaders allowed the teacher to continue to hold students to higher expectations.

One aspect of our definition of rigor is the notion of increased support for student learning. Rather than simply raising the bar, we contend that truly rigorous schools also support students as they move to higher levels. Too often, we say we provide support for students, but that is not always the case. As one principal described during our research:

> I don't think you can talk about high expectations without concurrently talking about how these expectations will be supported. Too often, the "high expectation" part is the emphasis because it plays better in the press and that rhetoric is easily compared with figuring out how you will support these expectations.

The most common approach for providing additional support is to provide extra help or tutoring sessions. By offering assistance to individual students or small groups in addition to regular classroom time, students can be more successful. However, this assistance is often optional and is most commonly scheduled after the regular school day. There are several challenges with this approach. First, when extra help occurs outside of the regular school day, some students who need assistance are unable to attend due to a lack of transportation.

Second, when extra help is optional, the students who need the most help do not seek it out. Many do not even realize they need help. As one student told us, *I don't go to that stuff. I either get it or I don't.* This reflects a lack of understanding of the role of effort.

In *Classroom Instruction that Works*, Marzano, Pickering, and Pollock (2001) make two important comments about students' views about effort.

Research-Based Generalizations About Effort

1. Not all students realize the importance of believing in effort.
2. Students can learn to change their beliefs to an emphasis on effort.

From: Marzano, et al., 2001, p. 50.

Although there are clear classroom-based implications from this research, from a school-wide perspective, it provides a direction for extra help opportunities. The students, who need the most help, often are the least likely to seek it out. Making extra help sessions mandatory, rather than optional, encourages a culture that says, "learning is not optional. We will insist that we work together so you can learn."

A principal in one of our workshops describes the lessons his/her faculty learned about extra support for students.

> We are working toward a mandatory approach beginning next school year for academic support in math and literacy. This year the program was strongly encouraged, but parents could opt out. Next year it will also be offered in both areas to students who need it in both . . . this year students get assistance in one area or the other.

Leadership in Action: Shifting the Culture

In Tucson, Arizona Pueblo High School serves a largely Hispanic population of 1900 students. It has a large English as a Secondary Language population and is situated in a high poverty neighborhood. When Pat Dienz became principal she found a school that needed rejuvenation. She described the school this way, "We needed to find a way to serve all of our students, to focus on student success, and to change the way we did things."

One thing that changed immediately was the way the principal talked about students and staff. Pat recognized the power of the stories she told to shape the culture of her school. She began to recognize

---

teachers who "went over and above to help students." She also identified a core of teachers who shared her vision and were willing to work with her to change many of Pueblo's routines.

Of particular concern were the acceptance of student failure, lack of rigor, and the unwillingness to change instructional practices. Pat began by focusing on improved instruction. She provided professional development for interested teachers and began a process to eliminate D's and E's, focusing on mastery with a revise-and-resubmit policy and creating a testing center where students could re-take tests. She also launched an initiative to use the school's advisory program as a tool to promote student success. The program name changed to A.C.I. for Academic Check-In. This simple modification sent a powerful signal that advisory had a different focus.

A. C. I. groups consist of 20-25 students who work with one of their teachers. The time is used for Sustained Silent Reading and other forms of academic support. A testing center was created where students can go to take tests missed when absent or re-take tests on which they were not successful. Students are also encouraged to "travel" to work with other teachers for tutoring or to make up missed work.

These changes didn't come about easily. In addition to telling stories about teacher leaders, Pat also began to recognize and talk about students who made significant changes in their academic success. More importantly, she persevered, recognizing that change does not occur quickly.

This principal recognized the power of stories, symbols, and routines to shape the way her school operated. She used the elements of culture to change the use of time and the commitment to student success.

Final Thoughts

As we said earlier, the culture of a school is a powerful tool for shaping the behavior of those who work and attend the school. It is important that principals recognize the way they can use the elements of culture to improve their school's commitment to rigor.

6

Ownership and Shared Vision

Any initiative to increase rigor requires the involvement of families and community as well as teachers and other school staff. Thus, it is important to involve all stakeholders in any formal discussions about increasing rigor in your school.

When teachers and others collaborate on instructional issues, their practice changes (Borko, 2004). Engaging all of the critical stakeholders at your school in efforts to improve rigor will strengthen their collective commitment to the change (David, 2009; Hord, 2009).

About a decade ago Ron and Howard Johnston from the University of South Florida began a study in four communities about increasing rigor in middle schools (Johnston & Williamson, 1998). As part of their research they asked parents, teachers, and students to think about a time when they felt challenged and involved in a rigorous activity. Everyone was asked to describe the experience, the feelings they had at the time of the experience, and the feelings they had as they recalled the experience.

From this study Ron and Howard found that school personnel and parents held different perspectives on rigor. Often teachers described school rigor as doing more of what they were currently doing—more reading, more projects, more papers. Parents, on the other hand, said that rigor was doing fewer things but going more in depth, exploring the implications of ideas, synthesizing learning, and generating hypotheses. Obviously, not every parent or every teacher fit this description. But the patterns were clear. Not everyone agrees on what constitutes rigor.

Characteristics of a Rigorous Task

- ◆ Rigorous tasks were authentic. They were performance-based and required a product, exhibit, or demonstration. There was often no clear path to completion and required use of skills in a new setting.
- ◆ Rigorous tasks were also thoughtful and reflective. They required synthesizing information, perhaps suspending or challenging old beliefs or habits. Almost always there was no single right answer.
- ◆ Rigorous tasks were often uncomfortable when being completed because of the possibility of failure and uncertainty of the outcome. They were also described as exhaustive but felt good when completed. Often people said they did things they may never have done before.
- ◆ Rigorous tasks were also individual. The task frequently varied but always involved passion about completion. Invariably people described the presence of high trust and high support.

From: Johnston & Williamson, 1998.

It reminds us of an experience we had looking at several pieces of art. We couldn't agree on their meaning or on their value. One friend said he couldn't define art but he sure knew it when he saw it.

It's much the same with rigor. People often can't define it but they sure recognize it when they see it.

Because of the varying perspectives about rigor, we've found that it is important to involve teachers, parents, and other appropriate stakeholders in any discussion about increasing rigor in your school. Be sure to include every group that has a role in the successful launch of any change. Chapter Nine will explore advocacy efforts in more detail.

Benefits of Cultivating Ownership

Involving others in decisions about making your school more rigorous is essential. It is important to have a broad base of support from all of a school's key stakeholder groups—teachers and staff, parents, and community.

Facilitators and Barriers to Cultivating Ownership	
Facilitators	*Barriers*
◆ Adequate time to meet; talk about rigor; plan, implement, and assess current efforts; lots of time may be required initially to get started ◆ Clear understanding of the areas/topics that the group can address ◆ Appropriate, ongoing professional development for all stakeholders, including conflict management and decision-making skills ◆ Accountability and responsibility of participants ◆ Availability of technical assistance ◆ Comfort and support of the principal	◆ Little or no professional development provided about collaborative work ◆ Limits of decision-making authority are unclear or undefined ◆ Principal directs and tells rather than guides ◆ Only the principal or superintendent is held accountable for decisions ◆ Group does not have power to make "real" decisions and gets mired in unimportant details

There is no formula for the perfect way to engage stakeholders in the discussion about rigor; however, authentic involvement around real tasks is important.

Sample Tasks
◆ Compare student work samples with agreed upon rubric
◆ Benchmark the curriculum to outside standards
◆ Interview parents and students about their perceptions of rigor

Most schools have groups that already provide input into decision-making—the School Improvement Team, a Principal's Advisory Committee, or a Professional Development Committee. You may want to involve these groups or you may want to create a special work group to guide your efforts.

Regardless, we have found that there are several important things that you should consider.

1. Who will be involved?
2. How will you form your team?
3. What contributions can individuals make? What is their level of expertise?
4. How will the team work together?

Determining Involvement

If people have a stake in the outcome of the decision and have some level of expertise, they should be involved. If an individual is indifferent to the outcome or has no expertise, no involvement is needed. Finally, if people have concerns about the outcome, but lack expertise, then they should have limited participation.

How to Determine Involvement	
Involve	Does this person have a stake in the outcome and have some level of expertise?
Don't Involve	Is this person indifferent to the outcome and have no expertise?
Limited Involvement	Does the person have concerns about the outcome but lacks expertise or is indifferent to the outcome?

Adapted From: Hoy and Tarter (2008).

Forming the Team and Getting Started

Other things to consider include clarity of the task and how the group will be organized and decisions made.

Checklist for Formation of Collaboration Teams
_____ Is the purpose clear? Is the role well defined?
_____ Is membership representative? Is membership appropriate to the task?

_____	Are there agreed upon norms for operation? For decision-making?
_____	Is there a mechanism to communicate with the larger school community? With other decision-making groups?
_____	What is the process for concluding the team's work?

From: Williamson and Blackburn (2009).

Reduce Isolation and Build Collaborative Relationships

We believe in the power of collaborative groups to positively impact schools. To assure greater success, a common base of information should guide every conversation about rigor. That means that family members are often working with teachers and principals on school improvement teams.

In some groups families and community members feel that teachers and principals have a greater voice in decisions and may have access to more information than they do. It is important to minimize these feelings by creating a culture where everyone has access to the same information. For example, everyone might be provided the same reading and then the group might spend time discussing the reading. Or you might ask everyone to review the same research from a recognized source like the College Board, or the Southern Regional Education Board (SREB).

Developing a Shared Vision of a Rigorous School

One of the most important things you can do as a leader is have a clear vision for your school. The North Central Regional Laboratory (2008) identified a "clear, strong and collectively held vision" as one of the six critical components of an effective school.

Beyond a general vision for your school, it is important that you and your teachers have a shared vision for a more rigorous school and classrooms.

Describing one's personal vision is not easy. Because it reflects our most intimate beliefs about life and about our work, preparing a statement of personal vision can be incredibly difficult. In their book on ethical leadership and decision-making, Joan Shapiro and Jacqueline Stefkovich (2005) describe work on a personal vision, or ethic, as one of the most important things a leader can do to be clear about what they value and about what is important in their school.

A Personal Vision of Rigor

Your personal vision consists of the most fundamental beliefs you hold about life, about your work, and about relationships with people.

A four-step process can be used to think about your own personal vision of a more rigorous school.

Developing a Personal Vision

Step 1: Think about your school. Make a list of what you would like to achieve as you make it more rigorous. Describe what it looks like and feels like.

Step 2: Consider the following things about what you have written—relationships, personal interests, and community. Examine each item in your list to ensure that it still fits.

Step 3: Develop a list of priorities. Identify the most important. Once this is done, review the list and rank them from most to least important. Remove the least important. Re-rank if appropriate. Check for relevance with your earlier list. Eliminate any item that is not relevant.

Step 4: Use the items from the first three steps to develop a personal vision statement. Review and edit the statement as often as needed until you believe it accurately reflects your commitment to more rigorous schools and classrooms.

Adapted from: Williamson & Blackburn (2009).

Vision Letters

A personal vision is also important for teachers and others who work in your school. While the beginning of the school year is a good time to invite teachers to consider their own personal vision, it can occur at any time.

In her book on classroom motivation Barbara (2005) recommends having teachers write vision letters. The letters provide teachers with an opportunity to consider the sort of classroom they want to create.

For example, ask teachers to imagine that it is the last day of school and to write a letter or e-mail to another teacher describing the past year—all that students accomplished, the rigor of their classroom, ways they supported student learning. Then ask teachers to describe how they plan to achieve their vision.

One principal we worked with asks teachers to write a vision letter at the start of every school year. Several times during the year they are asked to look at the letter and think about their progress toward making the vision a reality. This principal reports that it is a "really helpful motivational tool."

Another way to use the vision letter is to have teachers write the letter to you as principal. You can then use the letter as a part of a conversation with each teacher about his or her vision of a more rigorous classroom and how it relates to your vision of a more rigorous school.

Possessing a clear and compelling personal vision is important but not sufficient. Effective principals recognize the importance of working with staff and community to develop, nurture, and sustain a strong, collectively held vision for their school.

Thinking About a Shared Vision

When asking people to think about their shared vision it can be helpful to involve participants in a thoughtful, yet engaging activity. The principals we've worked with find this activity a fun way to launch the conversation about vision.

> Imagine you're hovering in a hot air balloon over your school and imagine it as rigorous as it might be—what would you see, what would you feel, what would you hear?

At one school the principal used a two-step process. First, she asked teachers to describe what they would currently see and hear in their school. Then they were asked to imagine it was five years in the future and to describe what they would see and hear from their hot-air balloon if their school were more rigorous.

Today	*Five Years from Today*

Creating or Recommitting to a School-Wide Vision

Effective principals recognize the importance of working with their school community to develop, nurture, and sustain a collectively held vision for their school.

Every school we've visited has a mission or vision statement. Many, however, are out-of-date and rarely used to set goals and priorities, allocation of resources, or make decisions about school programs. Even the clearest statements need periodic review. A review allows you to adjust the mission and vision based on up-to-date information about students and their needs. A review also allows the staff "to recommit to the school's core values and beliefs" (Williamson & Blackburn, 2009).

Process for Developing a School Vision Statement

Activity 1: What are the things people are pleased with and frustrated about at this school? (Designed to get the issues on the table.)

Activity 2: Invite the group to consider the values that should guide the school. You might ask, "As we begin planning for our future, what values are most important to you as we create our vision statement?" (Use of "I believe" statements focus on the important things.)

Note: A helpful approach is to have the group read some common things. For example, information about developmental needs of students, future trends, information about recommendations for schools at that level. Often professional associations (NASSP, ASCD) have useful resources. Shared readings create a common base of information and are particularly useful to minimize the barriers between teachers and parents where parents often defer to teachers as the "experts."

Activity 3: Ask the group to respond to the following: "Imagine it is the year 2012. We have been able to operationalize our beliefs. What does our school look, sound, and feel like? Describe the vision." (Helps to identify the target the school will work towards.)

Activity 4: In work groups develop a draft mission statement to be shared with the larger group. (Development of multiple models promotes discussion, clarification, and consensus building.)

Activity 5: Share the drafts, ask questions and seek clarification, and seek consensus on a statement. Plan to share it with the larger school community for feedback and comment.

From: Williamson & Blackburn (2009).

Vision is one of the most important components of an effective school. Being clear about your personal vision and working with others to be clear about the vision for your school, helps you and your faculty balance competing demands and make decisions based on your collective vision for your school.

District 102 outside of Chicago worked with Ron to develop their newly adopted vision statement for the middle grades.

District 102 Vision Statement

The vision of District 102's middle grades program is to prepare students intellectually and emotionally for personal and academic success in their school years and beyond. Our program's structure, organization, objectives, and goals will be based on the following values:

♦ a safe, supportive, and academically rigorous learning environment that meets the unique needs of our adolescent learners;
♦ the development of all students to their full potential;
♦ development of personal responsibility in all students;
♦ respectful relationships among students, staff, families, and community; and
♦ opportunities for exploration and expression for students across a broad range of disciplines.

Seeking Agreement About Decision on Rigor

Finally, dialogue with stakeholders to develop a clear definition of rigor and what rigor looks like linked to the research on rigor. The goal is to develop consensus about rigor in your school. It is essential that you engage everyone in the conversation. Seek to include every voice, particularly the missing voices of those who are often reluctant to speak out on issues. Welcome diverse ideas and give consideration to every one. It is critical to separate ideas from personalities and to be clear that once the faculty has decided on an approach, everyone is accountable for its implementation.

Although it is important to be clear about your vision for a rigorous school and classrooms, you must also be committed to working together to develop a mutually agreed upon vision for rigor.

Avoid voting on issues if at all possible. Voting creates an adversarial tone, one of winners and losers. Work to seek agreement. One tool we've found helpful to move a group toward consensus is the "Fist to Five" (Fletcher, 2002). When using the "Fist to Five," ask every participant to raise their hand and indicate their level of support, from a closed fist (no support) to all five fingers (it's a great idea). The "Fist to Five" technique is an easy way to determine the opinion of each person. It is a visible indicator of support and can help a group seek common ground. Many groups we've worked with continue the process until everyone holds up a minimum of three fingers.

Fist to Five	
Fist	No support—"I need to talk more on the proposal and require changes to support it."
1 Finger	No support but won't block—"I still need to discuss some issues and I will suggest changes that should be made."
2 Fingers	Minimal support—"I am moderately comfortable with the idea but would like to discuss some minor things."
3 Fingers	Neutral—"I'm not in total agreement but feel comfortable to let this idea pass without further discussion."
4 Fingers	Solid Support—"I think it's a good idea and will work for it.
5 Fingers	Strong Support—"It's a great idea and I will be one of those working to implement it."

Adapted From: Adventure Associates, 2009

Consensus does not mean that everyone has to agree with a decision. It does, however, mean that everyone in the group can support the decision—they agree they can live with it.

Leadership in Action

During the last year Ron has worked with the staff in District 102 outside of Chicago. They were committed to strengthening their middle grades program and created a study group that included teachers, administrators, and parents to look at the program.

They quickly found that individuals held starkly different visions for the school and its program. A process was designed to create a collectively agreed to statement of vision and several explicit supporting objectives. The group found that through their discussion about vision they developed greater understanding of the varying points-of-view.

Step 1:	Discuss current conditions (strengths and opportunities)
Step 2:	Use external facilitator to allow everyone to participate in the discussion
Step 3:	Identify areas of focus and provide evidence to support
Step 4:	Invite every member to suggest a statement of vision and supporting objectives and share with facilitator who synthesizes for the group
Step 5:	Share all proposed statements of vision with every member and ask for their feedback and suggestions
Step 6:	Meet and discuss the proposed vision and each proposed objective, agreeing to keep, merge, or discard based on level of support
Step 7:	Agree on vision and supporting objectives

Their adopted vision, shared earlier in this chapter, will serve to guide the further work at refining the program. Through these conversations about shared vision they cultivated a shared commitment to working together to improve the educational experience of students.

Final Thoughts

The most successful leaders are those that work with others to build a culture of continuous improvement. They recognize the importance of developing and nurturing a shared vision for their school and they value the participation of all stakeholders in decisions about their school's program.

7

Managing Data

A critical aspect of your journey to increase rigor is to appropriately manage data. Many principals are overwhelmed with the sheer amount of data they have and unsure how to use the information.

We want to be clear about what we mean by data. We're talking about all of the information you have, or you might collect, that will guide your work with teachers to make your school more rigorous. We believe that data is an important tool to guide decision-making, to measure success, and to monitor accountability. Our focus is on the use of data to help improve your school's program, not on data as an evaluative tool.

In this chapter, we'll use a four-step approach to demonstrate how data can support your effort to improve the rigor of your school.

Four Step Approach

1. Determine what you want to know
2. Decide how you will collect the data
3. Analyze the data/results
4. Set priorities and goals based on the analysis

From: Williamson and Blackburn (2009)

Step 1: Determine What You Want to Know

Be clear about what you want to know. Do you have questions about your school's program? About its success with students? About parent and community support? About the rigor in your classrooms?

Clarity about what you want to know can help you be clear about the data your might collect and analyze. In other words, what is your purpose for collecting and using data? You'll find that for each of the COMPASS tools, we'll repeatedly focus on clarity of purpose. That is because without a clear focus on why you are using each tool and how those tools support improvements in your school they simply become activities—things to do.

As with each of the tools, your purpose should be linked to the shared vision (see Chapter Six: Ownership and Shared Vision). We suggest that rather than just saying, "We want to increase rigor," you divide the task into smaller, more manageable chunks. For example, you might want to begin with a focus on one part of our definition of rigor (e.g., each student is expected to learn at high levels).

Possible Areas of Focus

- ◆ Expectations for Student Learning
- ◆ Support for Student Learning
- ◆ Demonstration of Student Learning
- ◆ Overall Culture of School Related to Rigor

As you narrow your focus you may identify several areas of concern. We've found that the most successful schools are those in which becoming more rigorous is a journey rather than an event. They select an initial area for improvement and put energy into it prior to moving to other areas.

There are many places to begin—curriculum, instruction, assessment, school environment. We've identified some characteristics of a rigorous curriculum, rigorous instruction, rigorous assessment, and a school community supportive of rigor.

Sample Characteristics for Expectations of Student Learning	
Curriculum	◆ Curriculum reflects new learning for students ◆ Curriculum is aligned with national and international standards

	◆ Curriculum incorporates higher order thinking skills ◆ Curriculum focuses on application of knowledge ◆ Factual, knowledge-based information is applied ◆ Curriculum offers opportunities for students to see relevance to their own lives and to the real world
Instruction	◆ Instruction offers opportunities for all students to engage in learning at high levels demonstrating that all students are expected to answer ◆ Instruction focuses on higher levels of questioning ◆ Review of basic information is streamlined and taught in a new manner ◆ Opportunities for application of learning are incorporated throughout the lesson ◆ Teacher wait time reflects the belief that all students are expected to answer
Assessment	◆ Assessment of learning is varied and includes performance-based aspects ◆ Assessments are structured so that students are given multiple opportunities for success ◆ Grading reflects a belief that it is mandatory to demonstrate learning
School Environment	◆ Everyone involved in the school environment encourages students to perform at high levels ◆ Everyone involved in the school environment models continual learning ◆ Teachers and other staff support one another's initiatives to improve teaching and learning ◆ Shared goals focused on student learning are used to assess new ideas and practices

Step 2: Decide How You Will Collect Data

Once you've determined an area of focus you will want to think about the data you already have. Many schools routinely gather data of all sorts. Think about what you already have and how it might be used to guide your work.

Data Frequently Available

- ◆ Student grades or test scores
- ◆ Student, parent, and staff surveys
- ◆ School climate data
- ◆ Instructional practices data
- ◆ Curriculum audit results
- ◆ Analysis of rigor by external evaluator
- ◆ Report of alignment with state or national standards

You may find that some of these data are helpful but that you need additional, more targeted data to give you the information needed to support your work. There are a variety of types of data you can collect. First, consider the types of data and determine which types of data will provide the information you need.

Types of Data

Demographic Data: These data describe the students and are most often used to understand the student learning data. It provides insight into equity among students.

Achievement and Learning Data: These data tell us what is going on in a school or district. They tell us what students learned and what they achieved. These data help us understand how students are achieving. Specific, disaggregated test item analyses provide insights into "what students got."

Instructional Process Data: These are the data that help you understand why students achieved at the level that they did. If reading scores are low, you might look at the type of reading students do, the time they spend on reading, the alignment of your reading program with state and local standards or benchmarks. These data also provide insights into why students in some classes learn and others may not. For example, teachers who participated in the recent training on the reading program achieve higher than students of teachers who did not participate.

Attitudinal Data: These data tell you about how people feel about a program, about how they experience your school or district program. Attitudinal or perception data will reveal "how they feel or what they believe about it."

From: Williamson & Blackburn, 2009.

When considering the data you may need to collect, build on your purposes. We've found that it may be helpful to phrase your issue as a question. Then, consider what data you already have and what types of data you would like to collect. Again, you likely have data readily available to you. Examples include test score data, enrollment in classes, parent or student survey results, attendance patterns, and requests to drop/add classes and/or teachers.

Data Collection		
Purpose: Does the instruction at _____ School reflect a belief that all students can learn at high levels?		
Data Type	*Available Existing Data*	*Data to Collect*
Demographic Data		
Achievement and Learning Data		
Instructional Process Data		
Attitudinal Data		

Ways to Collect Data

There are many different ways to collect data. It is helpful to include a mix of quantitative measures and qualitative measures. For example, student grades and test scores might be complemented by open-ended surveys or focus group conversations.

You may want to collect data on the curriculum that is in place, the instructional practices in your building, the assessments used to measure student learning, or the overall environment or school culture. Some of the tools we will suggest fit more than one category; others best fit just one area. Of most importance is that the data collection tool aligns with the area on which you are focusing.

Suggested Data Collection Tools	
Curriculum	◆ Comparison of curriculum to outside benchmarks (see Chapter Eight: Professional Development for process) ◆ Review of curriculum maps and/or pacing guides ◆ Prioritization of vocabulary or standards internally and externally (need to put this process somewhere) ◆ Analysis of test scores ◆ Comparison to NAEP scores ◆ Rubrics (self-assessment)
Instruction	◆ Classroom walkthroughs ◆ Lesson plan comparisons ◆ Student shadow studies ◆ Rubrics (self-assessment)
Assessment	◆ Comparison of grades to standardized test scores ◆ Rubrics (self-assessment) ◆ Comparison of levels of questioning ◆ Comparison of tests
Environment	◆ Governance Plan ◆ School Climate Assessment ◆ Community Involvement Plans

Data Collection Tools

You may also want to gather other data about rigor in your school and classrooms. There are several tools that may be used to collect information about current conditions. They include use of a rubric, facilitating focus group sessions, organizing an instructional walk-through, looking at student work, a curriculum comparison, or lesson study.

Use a Rubric

An effective way to gather data about how teachers or other members of the school community think your school is doing is through the use of rubrics. First, you need a clear, detailed rubric that is customized to the specific area or areas you want to assess. Next, introduce the rubric categories to your faculty. You might want to organize teachers into small groups and ask them to describe what each item would look like in a classroom. Ask them to compare their perspectives with a standard set of descriptors, such as the ones in this sample.

Sample Rubric Related to Instruction

Instruction: The school staff utilizes a range of instructional strategies that focus on student success and high expectations for the learning of all students.

At this school we ...	Maintain high expectations for learning	Include support and scaffolding in classroom instruction
High	Teachers act consistently on the unwavering belief that each student can learn, will learn, and their power to help them do so.	Teachers regularly provide the support and scaffolding each student needs to ensure their success. The support is customized for each student and affirms the belief that students are not allowed to not learn.
Medium	Teachers believe that each student can learn and that they can help them do so. They sometimes act on those beliefs or act on those beliefs with some students.	Teachers provide support and scaffolding for students to ensure their success. The support is customized for each student some times. At times, optional extra help is provided.

Sample Rubric Related to Instruction (continued)		
Low	Teachers are working to understand what it means that each student can learn, will learn, and they can help them do so.	Teachers sometimes provide support and scaffolding. The support is general and built into the regular lesson. At times, optional extra help is provided.

Finally, ask each member of your faculty to assess the school in each category, using the descriptors as a guide. However, it's also important to ask them to provide evidence for the ranking they choose. This will provide more detailed information for follow-up discussions.

Descriptor	Ranking	Evidence
Maintain high expectations for learning		
Include support and scaffolding in classroom instruction		

One way to use a rubric is for an internal self-assessment. But internal assessments are often inflated, may not accurately reflect what is really going on, or lack credibility with parents and other external groups.

Another way to use a rubric is to have someone knowledgeable in rigorous schools and classrooms conduct an assessment. They can use an established rubric to measure your school's current status and progress at becoming more rigorous. Assessments conducted by experts in the area, external to the school, frequently have much greater credibility and can help to identify a school improvement agenda.

Focus Group Meetings

Another strategy for gathering data about your school is to hold a series of focus group sessions with students, parents, teachers, or other interested people. A focus group is a group of individuals brought together to participate in a guided discussion about an issue of interest. The focus group can help you understand how members of the group experience the issue.

Focus group sessions consist of structured discussion and are generally most useful when conducted by an outside facilitator. This encourages participants to speak more freely and discuss difficult issues. The information that emerges should be scripted, analyzed for patterns and themes, and publicly reported and discussed.

When you arrange for a focus group, be clear about the purpose of the meeting. Most often, the purpose is to understand stakeholders' needs and to gather data about the current status of the school or a specific program related to rigor. Explain that data will not be identified with an individual and that only themes will be reported, which allows for limited individual confidentiality. Prior to the meeting, develop and use a set of guiding questions to start the discussion. Finally, always follow up responses with requests for more detail and information. It is usually helpful to ask for an example that illustrates the thinking.

Examples of Guiding Questions or Probes for Focus Groups

General:
+ Talk with me about your school. What's most important for me to know?
+ What are the school's strengths? Its challenges?
+ Describe your experience with this school.
+ What qualities define a successful _____ school?
+ Discuss this school's curriculum.

Specific:
+ Talk about experiences you've had that you described as rigorous. What was going on? Why was it rigorous?
+ When you feel really supported in your learning (or your student feels supported in his/her learning), what is happening?
+ How would you describe the rigor of this school's curriculum? What are examples of a rigorous classroom experience?
+ Discuss the expectations teachers have for student learning.
+ What suggestions do you have for strengthening our instruction to assure a more rigorous experience for students?
+ If you could change one thing at this school, what would it be? Please explain.

Other Questions You Would Like to Ask:

Instructional Walkthrough

Another way to gather data about the rigor in your school is to conduct an instructional walkthrough. We do not suggest a quick tour of the school but rather a focused visit to your school's instructional areas to collect information about your school's program.

Recently, many of the teachers and principals we work with chuckle when we mention a walkthrough. Where a walkthrough is compulsory or part of an evaluation system, they tend to be less successful.

When designed and implemented in a collaborative way walkthroughs can be a useful tool for getting information about your school. Based on our experience in schools we suggest the following steps for a successful walkthrough.

Prior to Conducting the Walkthrough

Establish a clear purpose for conducting a walkthrough. For example, it might be used to see how information from a recent Professional Development Workshop or Institute is used; gather data about implementation of a single instructional practice or learn about the presence of a single indicator of rigor.

Inform and prepare teachers. Regardless of the purpose, inform all teachers about, and prepare them for, the visit. They need to know who will be visiting, what data will be collected, and how the data will be shared and used following the walkthrough. Encourage teachers to conduct classes as they normally would, essentially ignoring the visitors and not interrupting routines. This is very important because a successful walkthrough collects data about current programs and practices. The walkthrough should not become a special event with specially designed lessons or activities.

Develop a plan for how observers will move throughout the school. This allows observers the opportunity to visit all instructional settings, rather than focusing on just one area. It may be appropriate to observe on more than one day and/or at various times throughout the day in the same classroom or instructional area.

Finally, identify the time needed to observe. Determine the amount of time for observation in each setting. The amount of time will depend on the observers' needs to get an accurate view of the instructional activity. Ensure that observers have the materials they need for recording their observations.

Leadership in Action

Area 10 of the Chicago Public Schools developed an instructional walkthrough process for collecting information about classroom instruction. Trinidad Liberto, Management Support Director for Area 10, described their "Instructional Rounds" process. Teams are created that include classroom teachers, a school coach and administrator. Each team of three or four people visits classrooms for thirty minutes. During the visits team members scribe what the teacher and students are doing and saying and complete a "Data Gathering Form." The process is repeated in several classrooms. The data is analyzed to look for common findings and develop an action plan.

Conducting the Walkthrough

Except in cases where classes may not be meeting, encourage observers to observe all instructional settings. Focus on the instructional practices present during the first few minutes of an observation. Data are recorded based on these initial observations.

While visiting classrooms, observers may want to talk with students. Responses from students can provide helpful information about your instructional program and expectations for students.

Possible Questions of Students

♦ What are you learning?

♦ Why do you need to know this information?

♦ What did you learn previously that helped you with this lesson?

♦ How do you know your work is good enough?

♦ If you want to make your work better, how do you know what to improve?

♦ What is an example of something you've done where you had to work hard but also learned a lot?

After observers make their observations, they should move from the setting to a place of privacy and discreetly record the information. Assure that the recording of each observation is anonymous. Observers want to get a view of instructional practice across the school, not in any particular classroom.

Following the Walkthrough

After gathering the data, provide an opportunity for all teachers to study the data and reflect on its meaning. Make all information collected available in an open and transparent way, one that invites conversation and discussion.

Engage teachers and other school personnel in conversation about the data, patterns that emerge, and meaning for their work together. Working with teacher leaders, develop a plan for this collaborative dialogue. Several formats might be considered, including:

- ♦ A discussion with the entire faculty
- ♦ Talking with a team or the faculty at one grade level or in one content area

Following the walkthrough, plan a debriefing with the observers. This meeting provides an opportunity to synthesize what was observed, to learn from other participants, and to deepen understanding of the instructional practices in your school. It also is a time to provide feedback to school personnel that will support continuous improvement.

Leadership in Action

At Aynor High School in Aynor, SC, teachers are able to participate in off campus learning walks. Kelly Johnson, Curriculum Specialist, says that the walks provide an opportunity for teachers to gather information about practices in other schools and that the process is less threatening when conducted off campus.

Curriculum Comparison

Another critical piece of data is an analysis of your curriculum. This may be a comparison to national or international benchmarks, or it may be an evaluation of curriculum by teachers at higher or lower grade levels to provide a basis for a discussion of vertical alignment. We will address this process more thoroughly in Chapter Eight: Professional Development.

Lesson Study

One way to gather data about the curriculum is to organize lesson study groups. Lesson study involves groups of teachers in a process to collaboratively develop lessons, teach the lesson, and then meet to discuss the lesson and its success and to plan for follow-up activities. The goal is to work together to develop, test, and refine instructional activities focused on rigor in your school. For example, the focus might be on expectations for students or opportunities to revise and resubmit student work.

Researchers from the University of Wyoming identified several positive benefits. They include the collaborative nature of the work, the sustained and on-going process, and how the way the teacher voice is honored in the work. The model recognizes that a prescriptive "top-down" approach to school reform has not been effective.

Student Work

Finally, don't forget that a powerful source of information is student work. You might conduct a walkthrough with faculty to observe the school and student work or examine student work during grade-level, team, or department meetings. We'll also discuss this concept in more detail in Chapter Eight: Professional Development.

Collect Your Data

Next, collect data. You may simply need to locate readily available data or determine ways to gather local data about the focus area. Collected data should align with the data analysis questions. A crosswalk (see below) provides a visual tool to track the appropriate data to match each question.

Crosswalk			
Data Analysis Question	Does the instruction at _____ School reflect a belief that every student is expected to learn at high levels?	Are teachers persistent in supporting student learning?	Are students engaged in instructional activities that use high-order thinking?
Demographic Data			
Achievement and Learning Data			
Tracking Processes Data			
Attitudinal Data			

Step 3: Analyze the Data/Results

As you begin to analyze your data, be sure to involve all constituents in the process, which we discussed in Chapter Six: Ownership and Shared Vision. As you analyze the results of your data, it's important to keep an open mind rather than pre-determining the results. Otherwise, you may not see the full picture. First, analyze the information provided by each data source.

Data Source Analysis		
Data Source:		
Areas of Strength	*Areas for Potential Growth*	*Areas That Need More Information*

Then, look for patterns across multiple sources of data. This will allow you to prioritize action steps in areas that need the most work. You may find that you don't have enough data to select an area of focus. If so, consider how you might gather additional data.

Data Pattern Analysis			
Areas of Strength			
Focus Area	*Data Source 1*	*Data Source 2*	*Data Source 3*

Areas for Potential Growth			
Focus Area	Data Source 1	Data Source 2	Data Source 3
Areas That Need More Information			
Focus	Data Source 1	Data Source 2	Data Source 3

Many schools try to work on too many things at the same time. This dissipates the energy of teachers and administrators and may not provide the improvement you seek. A thorough pattern analysis will help you prioritize areas for improvement. Although you will want to involve teachers in the data analysis process, at some point the data must be shared with a larger audience, whether that is all teachers, or stakeholder groups. Planning thoughtfully and purposefully for the discussion is foundational for positive growth. One of the lessons we've learned about presenting and using data is the importance of presenting data in a non-threatening way in order to ensure purposeful engagement. Rather than discussing areas of concern, we've termed it areas for potential growth.

Force Field Analysis

A force field analysis is a tool for diagnosing situations, and it can provide clear guidelines for action. The process works well with small as well as large groups and provides an opportunity to examine both facilitators and inhibitors of change.

To do so, consider both driving forces and restraining forces that are helping or hurting your efforts to increase rigor. Driving forces are those forces affecting a situation that are pushing in a particular direction; they tend to initiate a change and keep it going. Restraining forces are forces acting to restrain or decrease the driving forces.

Sample Driving Forces	Sample Restraining Forces
◆ Data about student learning ◆ Demographic data ◆ Number of students who drop out of college after graduating from your high school ◆ Data from local employers about numbers of new employees who need basic retraining	◆ Belief that some students can't achieve at high levels ◆ Pressure from parents for students to make all A's ◆ Apathy ◆ Contractual issues ◆ Costs of an innovation

Using the Force Field Analysis

Once you have decided to increase the rigor in your school, a force field analysis allows you to look at all the forces for or against your initiative. It helps you to plan for or reduce the impact of the opposing forces and strengthen and reinforce the supporting forces.

In order to conduct a force field analysis, state the problem or desired state in clear, concrete terms. Next, discuss and identify the factors that are working for and against the desired state.

Factors Working For	Factors Working Against

Third, review and clarify each factor. Once you agree on the list of factors, determine the strength of each factor. For example, assign a score to each force, from 1 (weak) to 5 (strong) or high, medium, or low. Finally, discuss the factors and their scores to identify appropriate next steps. Those factors working against the desired state may become the focus of plans of action. This information will help you set your priorities and goals.

Step 4: Set Priorities and Goals

Finally, work with your School Improvement Team or other collaborative group to determine priorities based on your area of focus and your data analysis.

Once you have determined your priorities, goals, or area of focus, study and select strategies that will allow you to address the area of focus. This is a pivotal point. Too often, we gather and analyze data, set goals, but then do not use that information to make decisions on an ongoing basis. We've developed an action planning process for the use of DATA.

Action Planning Process

Data Source(s)
- Areas for Potential Growth
- Tracking Success
- Action Steps

Using your pattern analysis, note the data sources you used. Next, identify the area for potential growth, such as incorporating more activities in which each student is required to demonstrate learning. Third, design a specific way to track success. How will everyone know if they are making progress toward the goal? What does success look like? Finally, detail the specific action steps that are needed to accomplish the goal.

Action Plan Template for Use of Data		
Data Source(s)		
Area for Potential Growth	*Indicators for Tracking Success*	*Action Steps*

Final Thoughts

Gathering and using data to guide decisions about improving the rigor of your school is important. Be cautious about simply gathering data. The value of data is in its analysis and use to help select improvement strategies and monitor your progress in meeting your improvement goals.

Principals who are most successful use data routinely to guide their work, but they recognize that it is vitally important to involve teachers, staff, and families in both the collection and use of the data.

8

Professional Development

Effective professional development can facilitate your efforts toward increased rigor. Contemporary professional development moves beyond the traditional activities such as seminars, workshops, courses, and conferences to encompass a wider variety of activities, including inquiry action research projects, book study groups, mentoring, peer coaching, and collaborative work teams.

Contemporary Professional Development

According to the National Staff Development Council (http://www.nsdc.org), contemporary professional development should have three defining characteristics:

1. Results Driven
2. Standards Based
3. Job Embedded

In other words, professional development should follow a path that leads to clear results. Activities should be based on standards, and they should be thoroughly woven into the job, rather than simply being an activity that is done as an "extra," possibly outside of work hours or the work experience.

Key Lessons from Award-Winning Schools

Based on our research with schools that won the U. S. Department of Education's Award for Staff Development (Blackburn, 2000), we found seven key elements of effective staff development.

Key Elements of Effective Staff Development

1. Clear purpose linked to research, student data, goals, and needs
2. Accountability through classroom use of ideas and impact on students
3. Development of a common, shared language
4. Shared decision-making that includes an emphasis on teacher input
5. Incorporation of relevant, practical, hands-on activities
6. Integration of opportunities for follow-up and application
7. Strong leadership and a positive, collegial atmosphere

How do these elements support your efforts toward increased rigor?

First, you should have a clear purpose that is linked to research, student data, goals, and needs. Specifically, what area or areas of rigor do you want to improve? Is there research to support your plan? Is the planned initiative justified based on the data in terms of test scores, student surveys and feedback, or some other type of data (see Chapter Seven: Managing Data)? Does it align with the goals of your school? Finally, does it meet a need in your school?

The second key element is accountability in terms of classroom use and student results. Without accountability, you will likely not see a lasting impact. The first aspect of accountability is simple: how will the information about rigor be used in the classroom? If your teachers are reading *Rigor is NOT a Four-Letter Word,* are they expected to try at least one strategy from each chapter? Will you look at student work in order to ensure use (see Chapter Nine: Shared Accountability)? Interestingly, the teachers in the study were the strongest advocates for principals holding them accountable for classroom use.

Next, consider student results. As an outcome of the planned professional development, what do you actually see in terms of the impact on students? How will you know that students will benefit from the work on rigor? Once again, although this can include test scores, you may also see impact through increased student engagement, more students revising work for a higher grade, or an increase in the amount of students choosing higher levels of coursework.

The third key element is the development of a common shared language. When you use your professional development to develop a consistent frame of reference for rigorous expectations, higher levels of student engagement, or increased support for student learning, it helps provide a focus for all stakeholders.

Why should I care about a common, shared language?
A common, shared language exists when all stakeholders describe a concept similarly. For example, effective professional development helps everyone understand what rigor is, what it is not, and shared indicators of progress.

Fourth, if you want to increase the effectiveness of your professional development, create shared governance that includes teacher input. This is more than just surveying teachers and asking them about their interests. Rather, create ways for teachers to be truly involved in the decision-making that goes along with professional development. You'll find specific strategies in Chapter Six: Ownership and Shared Vision.

The next key element is relevant practical hands-on activities. Are your professional development activities relevant to the stakeholders? Is there a practical value that is perceived by all participants? Are they allowed to interact in ways that increase engagement? We want rigor that is motivating and engaging for students. Why would we expect less for our teachers?

The sixth element is follow up. A quick, one-time activity will not produce lasting results. How are you incorporating follow up at every stage? What are the expectations for participants after the activity? Do you ask each teacher to complete an action plan? When we speak, we finish each session by asking participants to define one next action they plan to complete in order to increase rigor in their setting when they return to their schools and/or classrooms. Again, you'll find a more thorough discussion of accountability in Chapter Ten.

Finally, strong leadership is crucial to any effective professional development. Throughout this book, we've provided tools that will help you lead effectively. However, leadership includes more than just the administrators in a building. It also includes teacher leadership, which we discussed in Chapter Six: Ownership and Shared Vision.

But without your leadership, a plan fails. A Texas principal we met provided an avenue to build teacher leadership for professional development in his school. Instead of having two regular faculty meetings each month, he shifted one to professional development for teachers. Focused on the topic of rigor, teachers could share what they learned at a conference, something they had read, or a new strategy they were implementing in their classroom. Although it took time, teachers became comfortable sharing their own practice, and they soon began asking to do the same in the second meeting.

Directly linked to leadership are the positive attitudinal elements in the school. How open are you, your administrators, and teachers to sharing learning? What is the willingness factor, the desire to collaboratively work together to increase rigor throughout the school? This truly reflects the culture of your school (see Chapter Five: Culture) and is a direct result of your leadership in this area.

By weaving these characteristics together, your professional development will strengthen your efforts to create a rigorous school environment. Let's look at two practical strategies that incorporate these characteristics: professional learning communities and looking at student work.

Professional Learning Communities

One effective professional development tool is a "professional learning community." The term has become commonplace and is used to mean almost any sort of collaborative work. Richard DuFour (http://www.bpe.org/documents/DuFour-WhatarePLCs.pdf) says," the term has been used so ubiquitously that it is in danger of losing all meaning."

The professional community of learners originally suggested by Astuto and colleagues (1993) talks about a school where teachers and administration continuously seek and share learning and act on what they learn. The goal is to improve effectiveness focused on improving the learning of students. Overall, effective learning communities have three defining characteristics.

Defining Characteristics of PLCs

- Ensuring that students learn
- A culture of collaboration
- A focus on results (whatever it takes)

In order to build a successful learning community, you must abandon the traditional position of authority and become an active participant in your own professional development and that of teachers. Your role is that of a learner, along with teachers and other staff, "questioning, investigating, and seeking solutions for school improvement" (Hord, 1997). Next, to set aside the traditional hierarchy and recognize there is a need for everyone to contribute, you must be skillful at facilitating the work of staff. Respecting the inquiry process, promoting understanding, and constructing mutually agreed upon solutions, you will need to participate without dominating.

Leadership in Action: A Professional Learning Community Focused on Rigor

Curriculum Alignment/Adjustments

Central to the effectiveness of professional learning communities is their emphasis on student learning. Built around collaborative endeavor professional learning communities that lack a focus on learning fail to achieve all of the potential benefits. The focus must be on student learning rather than collaboration. Collaborative activity is the tool that enhances a staff's ability to make a difference in the achievement of students.

An important aspect of increasing rigor is evaluating the curriculum in your school. Chapter One: A Rationale for Rigor provided convincing reasons for taking this step in order to see the most long-term gains for students.

Leaders can use the following process with teachers to determine any adjustments that might be needed to your curriculum. Remember, in a professional learning community, the role of the leader is that of a facilitator, one who guides teachers, but does not force decisions. Ideally, you can group your teachers by subject area and include teachers from a range of grade levels. Including teachers from earlier grade levels and higher grade levels will inform your discussions.

Evaluating and Adjusting Curriculum

Providing Background Knowledge for the Discussion

1. In subject-specific groups, ask teachers to use post-it notes to draft all the topics, concepts, or standards they believe are important. Color-code this by grade level or course (it's easiest to use different colors of post-it notes).
2. Next, compare the notes to your actual state standards. What do teachers include that is not part of your standard? What is missing?
3. Find a set of national standards for comparison (see Recommended Resources for a starting point). Compare the state standards and the teachers' topic notes to the national standards. What is different?

**Leadership in Action: A Professional
Learning Community Focused on Rigor (continued)**

Linking the Research Base
1. Using the information from Chapter One: A Rationale for Rigor, discuss the research findings with all teachers. You may want to pull the original research for more information.
2. Ask teachers to compare those findings to what they discovered in their own comparison.

Taking the First Step
1. Now, move back into subject-specific groups. Ask teachers to develop a draft outline of content for the year that is aligned with national standards.
2. Sketch out a pacing guide that will allow for **necessary** review, but incorporates instruction that is more rigorous.

Implementation
1. Begin incorporating the new instruction.
2. Ensure appropriate vertical alignment.
3. Meet to discuss what is working and what needs to be changed.
4. Adjust as needed.

Using the example as a model, consider other ways that a professional learning community can support the move to a rigorous school. In addition to engaging teachers and staff in discussions about the curriculum, there are other things you can do to support professional learning communities.

**Structures that Facilitate
Professional Learning Communities**

- Build schedules and organizational structures that reduce isolation.
- Incorporate policies that encourage greater autonomy, foster collaboration, and enhance effective communication.
- Provide time for staff development within the regular school day.
- Work with faculty and staff to develop a willingness to accept feedback and work toward improvement.
- Be open to sharing professional practice.
- Create an atmosphere of trust and respect among colleagues.

Leadership in Action: Looking at Student Work

Another powerful way to improve your school's instructional program and to improve the educational experience of students is to look at authentic student work (see Chapter Seven: Managing Data). In many schools, teams of teachers, either at the departmental, course, or grade level, examine the work of students as a way to clarify their own standards for student work, to strengthen common expectations for students, or to align curriculum across faculty.

Looking at student work is a complex task that significantly alters the norms of a school. It necessitates a climate where faculty are comfortable sharing their work with colleagues and revealing artifacts about their classroom practice. The Annenberg Institute for School Reform suggests several preliminary steps.

Steps to Begin Looking at Student Work

- ♦ Talk together about the process and how to assure that it is not evaluative;
- ♦ Identify ways to gather relevant contextual information (e.g., copy of assignment, scoring guide, or rubric);
- ♦ Select a protocol or guideline for the conversation that promotes discussion and interaction;
- ♦ Agree on how to select work samples; and
- ♦ Establish a system for providing and receiving feedback that is constructive.

Step One: Align Expectations with High Standards

One purpose for looking at student work is to align teachers' expectations with standards. The first step is to define high quality. Rubrics are an effective way to determine expectations for quality. However, if you don't have anything for comparison, you may unknowingly lower your standards when developing a rubric. Using benchmarks allow you to frame the conversation through a lens of neutral standards rather than limiting the perspective to personal opinions.

The Southern Regional Education Board (SREB) offers detailed descriptions of proficiency levels tied to the National Assessment of Educational Progress (NAEP) test levels for student preparing to enter high school. One of the findings from SREB's research is that many teachers expect advanced students to perform at the proficient level and on-grade level students to perform at a basic level of competency. The charts below show sample expectations for students leaving the eighth grade.

Making Inferences and Predictions (Reading/Language Arts)		
Basic	Proficient	Advanced
◆ Identify an author's stated position. ◆ Make simple inferences about events and actions that have already occurred, characters' backgrounds, and setting. ◆ Predict the next action in a sequence.	◆ Use evidence from text to infer an author's unstated position. ◆ Identify cause and effect in fiction and nonfiction. ◆ Predict a character's behavior in a new situation, using details from the text. ◆ Formulate an appropriate question about causes or effects of actions.	◆ With evidence from a nonfiction piece, predict an author's view-point on a related topic. ◆ Describe the influence of an author's back-ground upon his/her work. ◆ Recognize allusions.

From: Southern Regional Education Board, 2004.

Gather, Organize, Display, and Interpret Data (Math/Algebra I)		
Basic	Proficient	Advanced
◆ Make and read single bar graphs, single line graphs, and pictographs. ◆ Read and interpret circle graphs.	◆ Read and make line plots and stem-and-leaf plots. ◆ Collect and display data for given situations.	◆ Formulate survey questions and collect data. ◆ Evaluate statistical claims in articles and advertising.

◆ Find the mean, median, mode, and range of sets of data. ◆ Plot points on a coordinate grid.	◆ Make, read, and interpret double bar, double line, and circle graphs. ◆ Determine when to use mean, median, mode, or range. ◆ Determine and explain situations of misleading statistics.	◆ Analyze different displays of the same data.

From: Southern Regional Education Board, 2004.

Describe Sound and Light in Terms of the Properties of Waves (Science)		
Basic	*Proficient*	*Advanced*
◆ Describe the electromagnetic spectrum. ◆ Demonstrate the characteristics of sound and light waves. ◆ Explain the effect of different media substances on wave transmission.	◆ Relate the electromagnetic spectrum to practical applications. ◆ Examine and relate characteristics of sound and light to wavelength, amplitude, and frequency. ◆ Research why different energy forms require a medium.	◆ Draw conclusions about natural phenomena based on the electromagnetic spectrum. ◆ Research and summarize the effects of surfaces on light and sound reflection and absorption. ◆ Research product designs that impact sound transmission.

From: Southern Regional Education Board, 2004.

There are a variety of other sources for standards for all grade levels, including the National Center on Education and the Economy's (NCEE)

Evaluating and Adjusting the Curriculum

Our Priority Topics	State Standards	National Standards

Areas that need more focus:

Areas that need less attention:

Other needed adjustments:

"New Standards" Performance Standards (http://www.ncee.org) and the new common, core standards (http://www.corestandards.org). Choose the national standards that are most helpful for your use.

Step Two: Develop Consistent Expectations

It's helpful to gauge expectations with published standard expectation levels, but it's also important to simply sit down with other teachers and administrators to discuss expectations. One way to start the conversation is to choose a standard assignment that students complete, such as writing a short essay. Share copies of the paper with a group and ask everyone to assess it. Since everyone participates, each teacher actually assesses a paper from each of the other teachers. If you do this by department, grade level, or team, you will probably have about five papers to assess. Meet to discuss the results. It's likely that some teachers will be more rigorous, and others less. However, as you talk about how you determine quality, you'll come to consensus about your expectations.

We recommend that you begin by structuring or guiding meetings among teachers of the same subject and grade level. Over time, extend the work to conversations across grade levels. Ask questions of teachers of higher grades such as, "What do you expect students to know before they come into your class? From your perspective, what are the overall strengths students bring into your classroom? What are some areas that students struggle with?" Then, meet with teachers one grade level below each teacher's level to discover new information to help guide instruction for the coming year.

Barbara was working with one district to address consistency across grade levels. A specific area of concern was the quality of students' responses on open-ended questions. Teachers at one of the middle schools explained that incoming sixth graders were ill-prepared for the level of work because "they are coming from elementary school and must adjust to our higher expectations." However, when she visited the feeder elementary school, fifth grade teachers told her, "we always assign open-ended questions and expect it to be completed. We want them to be ready for middle school." Because the teachers at each school had never met to discuss expectations, the sixth grade teachers had less rigorous requirements, but didn't realize it. The teachers and principals met together to ensure expectations were aligned.

PRESS Forward Model for Action Planning

All of the strategies we've shared can make a positive difference in your school. You will need to determine which ones may be most effective in your situation, and you'll likely need to customize them to your setting. For example, for the curriculum alignment activity, high school teachers tend to meet in departments, middle schools in teams, and elementary schools by grade levels. However, it is critical to start with a plan that incorporates the elements of effective professional development—focused on results, job embedded, and standards based.

In our PRESS Forward model, you design a plan that has a clear purpose, is related and connected to other aspects of your school community, has a set of clear outcomes and action steps, and describes the support that is needed to be successful. Our plan is cyclical, with benchmarks built in at each stage of the process that provide an opportunity for reflection before you move forward.

PRESS Forward	
Purpose	Why are we doing professional development on rigor?
Relationships and Connections	How does a focus on rigor relate to our mission, goals, and needs of our students? How does it connect with other initiatives in our school?
Expected Outcomes	If the professional development is affected, what changes will we see related to teachers' practice and student learning?
Steps to Take	What are the specific action steps we need to take to accomplish our goals? What is the timeline for each step?
Support Needed	What types of support do we need to accomplish each step? What material resources are necessary?
Forward	After a stage of implementation, take time to reflect, refine your plan, and move forward with next steps.

PRESS Forward Template

Purpose							
Relationships and Connections							
	Expected Outcomes	Steps to Take	Support Needed				
Forward Focus:							
	Next or Adjusted Expected Outcomes	Next or Adjusted Steps to Take	Support Needed				

Final Thoughts

A commitment to professional growth characterizes the most effective schools. Professional learning communities and other collaborative structures, provide a mechanism for teachers, principals, and other staff to make the improvement of student learning a priority.

As you work with your teachers to make your school more rigorous one of the most valuable tools is a focused, standards-based, high-quality professional development program.

9

Advocacy

School leaders are advocates, always advocating for their school and ways to improve the educational experience of students. It is one of your important roles. Advocacy is what you do when you are actively supporting a cause like increasing the rigor of your school. It is often compared to public relations. But advocacy is quite different. When a leader advocates for their program they are committed to providing information to stakeholder groups that will build support for their vision of increased rigor. They recognize the importance of building networks and alliances that will support their efforts

This chapter will discuss advocacy and provide you with several useful tools that you can use to develop your advocacy plan.

Why Be an Advocate?

Advocacy is a way to effectively press for change. It is also the foundation of our democracy and a process that allows ordinary people to shape and influence policy at all levels. Identifying priorities, crafting a strategy, taking action, and achieving results are critical steps to finding one's voice, making oneself heard, and shaping one's future.

In his recent book on future trends Gary Marx (2006) from the Educational Research Service described the trends shaping the work of school leaders. One of those trends was recognition that schools are interconnected with every facet of the community and the world. Marx suggests that the most successful leaders will be those who are skilled at working with others by building networks of support, creating alliances with other groups, and identifying ways to work cooperatively on shared interests.

School leaders can use these advocacy strategies to work with both internal and external constituents to create a climate supportive of increased rigor in schools.

Successful Advocates . . .

♦ Speak from the heart when telling their story
♦ Speak to the local impact and implications
♦ Are factual and honest
♦ Are clear, concise, and concrete
♦ Develop sound bites, success stories, elevator talks, and one-page fact sheets
♦ Frame the issue and tie it to a larger picture
♦ Are cheerfully persistent
♦ Know their audience and build their advocacy appropriately
♦ Don't forget to follow up and say thank you

First Steps

How do you respond to the need to build a network and advocate for your school's future? We've identified an eight-step process that can help you develop a plan to build support for your efforts to increase the rigor of your school.

Eight Step Planning Process

1. Analyze your environment: Scan the environment in which your school exists—district, community, state, nation, and world. Identify the issues that affect your school and those that affect your community more broadly.
2. Monitor changes in your environment: Read voraciously, talk with a wide selection of people in your community (see "movers and

---

shakers") and stay current with trends at the state and national level.

3. Identify the factors needed for success: Look beyond traditional factors (good teachers, money) and consider emerging issues such as the acquisition and use of technology, the ability to respond to changing conditions. Consider groups in your community with which you can partner.

4. Think about your assumptions: Identify the assumptions you hold about your school and its environment. Test them by assessing the degree of certainty (high, medium, low) and the level of impact (high, medium, low). Assumptions play an important role in constructing the future.

5. Develop a vision of an alternate future: Consider the issue of rigor at your school and identify the factors you identified are critical for success. Develop a vision of the future that is different from current circumstances. Creating several alternatives is better.

6. Consider allies and opponents: Identify individuals or groups that may support your efforts as well as those who may resist. Be sure and include those you know and those that may emerge. Develop a plan for building alliances with your allies and understand the opposition.

7. Develop a plan for advocating for your desired future: Identify specific steps that can be taken to achieve the anticipated future. Develop both "hedging strategies that can cope with undesirable futures and "shaping strategies; that help create the desired future.

Adapted from: Marx, 2006; Williamson and Blackburn, 2009.

Designing an Advocacy Plan

Similar to other planning efforts, crafting an advocacy plan includes several distinct steps. First and foremost as we discussed earlier, be clear about the issue (for example, increasing the rigor of instruction in classrooms at your school).

You also need to identify goals and accompanying strategies, know something about your allies and opponents and those who might emerge as allies or opponents, and develop advocacy strategies and identify opportunities. Finally, you need to implement your plan and monitor its results.

Stakeholders

Every school community has both internal and external stakeholders, people who have a "stake" in the success of your school. When developing a plan to advocate for your vision of a more rigorous school it may be easy to focus on the groups outside the school that need to be mobilized. But, it will also be necessary to engage and inform people who work in your school every day.

Stakeholder Groups	
Internal	*External*
◆ Teachers ◆ Other staff ◆ Students ◆ Administrative team	◆ Families ◆ School board ◆ Business leaders ◆ Senior citizens ◆ Neighbors without children in the school ◆ Media

The groups will have differing needs for information and you may need to develop several strategies to inform them of your work and engage them as partners in your advocacy efforts.

Internal Stakeholders

Throughout the book we've talked about ways to involve and inform internal groups. We won't repeat that information but we want to reinforce several key ideas.

First, it is important to recognize that everyone who works or attends your school may not have the same level of support for increasing rigor. Second, regardless of the level of support you must develop a plan to work with every staff member to build momentum toward your vision.

We've identified several important considerations about working with internal stakeholders.

Considerations for Working with Internal Stakeholders

♦ Create opportunities for teachers and other staff to be involved in planning to increase rigor;

♦ Provide multiple forms of professional development to help increase capacity for improving rigor;

♦ Communicate in a variety of ways;

♦ Engage both supporters and detractors in conversations about rigor and strategies for improving rigor in your school;

♦ Attend to your own professional growth and development about rigor;

♦ Model the use of rigor in your daily interactions with staff;

♦ Share examples of best practices from within your school and from other sites; and

♦ Don't expect that everyone will embrace your vision.

External Stakeholders

Schools do not exist in isolation. They are part of the fabric of every community and reflect community values and priorities. It is essential that school leaders work closely with external stakeholders to advocate for their school's vision of increased rigor.

The external community is comprised of groups with very different needs for information and access to the school. Here are a few important tips we've learned about advocacy and these external stakeholders.

Families There is no more important external group than the families of your students. Later in this chapter we will discuss the advocacy needs of families. It is important to involve families in school life through participation on School Improvement Teams, by communicating regularly, through opportunity for workshops and other family development activities, and by providing a healthy and supportive environment at home for students to prepare for school.

School Board Your local school board is an important external stakeholder group. They have an important governance role making decisions about the allocation of personnel and financial resources. Work with your superintendent and central office staff to identify ways for keeping your board informed about your school and your vision for improved rigor. Find a way to share vision and your successes. In an earlier chapter we described the "Turn-around" stories told by a Phoenix area principal. You may want to develop your own set of stories about your school that you can share both formally and informally with school board members. Invite them to visit your school. Let them see firsthand your progress at improving rigor. Encourage them to talk with teachers and students about their work.

Business Community Business leaders are strong advocates for effective schools because they hire school graduates. They are keenly aware of the importance of education, the skills needed for success in the workplace, and the need to stay up-to-date and current. Business leaders always want to be assured that your school has a business-like atmosphere, focused on teaching and learning, and one that provides "value" for the money spent on schools. Many school leaders find it useful to join local fraternal groups so that they can network with the business community and advocate for their school.

Senior Citizens It is important for school leaders to build connections to the senior community. Seniors vote more frequently than any other group. Increasingly, seniors are willing and able to provide tutoring and other support for school programs. They enjoy working with children and making a contribution to their community.

Neighbors of the School In most communities there are more people without children in schools than those with children in school. Neighbors of the school are an important group. They are invariably interested in your school's program and how it impacts their neighborhood. Many principals we've met find it important to network with homeowner's associations and other neighborhood groups.

Media Not a traditional stakeholder group, the media in many communities have the potential to positively impact your school's agenda. School leaders need to know who the key media voices are in their community and how to provide them with the information they need to get your school's message out to the larger community. In St. Louis, MO, Pam Hughes, principal of Metro High School, worked with a local television station to create a short segment of interest to parents that was part of the 6 a.m. newscast. It provided tips on handling homework, nutrition, parenting, and school activities.

Movers and Shakers

You may want to identify the "movers and shakers" in your school community, your district, and your state so that you can advocate for your vision of a more rigorous school.

Who are the "movers and shakers?" They are individuals who are recognized leaders in their area, those who others turn to for guidance on important issues. They are able to get things done by rallying support, identifying resources, and building coalitions.

Think about your own school. Who would you identify as a "mover and shaker"? He or she may be a parent but might also be someone who does not have children in your school.

Name the five "movers and shakers" in your school community.

1.
2.
3.
4.
5.

Now, think about your school district. Who are the "movers and shakers" in your district?

Name the five "movers and shakers" in your school district.

1.
2.
3.
4.
5.

Often the most influential "movers and shakers" reside beyond the boundaries of your school or district. They may be influential politicians, policy makers, or community development personnel.

Now that you have identified the "movers and shakers" consider why they were included in the list. Why are they a "mover and shaker"?

Build a Network

To be truly effective, you need to build a network of people who can help with your advocacy efforts. Remember, communication is a two-way street, so this group will serve two purposes: to help you understand how stakeholders in various groups perceive a situation and to help you communicate your message. There are actually several layers of this strategy. For example, if you lead a large school, you may use an existing leadership team to assist you in this area. In addition, you may want a network for parents, and another one for the business community. Or, you may want one network that incorporates all those groups.

One model is the Key Communicator Network, developed by the National School Public Relations Association. They recommend a series of steps for building a network and leading that group. As you work with stakeholders, there is one foundational point to remember: as the principal, you are the face of the group. Share responsibility but don't forget that in the eyes of the community you are responsible for getting things done and for sharing reliable and accurate information. Never create a situation where you compromise your beliefs about honesty and trustworthiness.

Building A Key Communicator Network

1. Bring together a small group of trusted people who know the community. Brainstorm with those whom others listen to. While the bank president may be an opinion leader, so might the barber, cab driver, bartender, or supermarket checkout clerk.

2. Create a workable list from all the names that have been gathered to invite to join your network. Make sure that all segments of the community are represented.

3. Send a letter to the potential members, explaining that you want to create a new communications group for your school to help the community understand the challenges, successes, and activities of your school. In the letter invite the potential members to an initial meeting and include a response form.

4. Make follow-up phone calls to those who do not return the response form, especially those who will be most important to have on your network.

5. Start the initial meeting by explaining that those in the audience have been invited because you see them as respected community members who care about the education students are being provided. Also, point out that you believe schools operate best when the community understands what is taking place and becomes involved in providing the best possible learning opportunities for students. Then, describe the objectives of a Key Communicator Network—

   ♦ To provide network members with honest, objective, consistent information about the school;

   ♦ To have the network members deliver this information to others in the community when they are asked questions or in other opportunities; and

   ♦ To keep their ears open for any questions or concerns community members might have about the school. Those concerns should be reported to the principal or person in charge of the network so communication efforts can deal with those concerns. (It's always best to learn about concerns when one or two people have them instead of when 20 or 30 are vocally sharing them with others.)

   Ask the invitees for a commitment to serve on the network and find out the best way to communicate with them, i.e. email, fax, and telephone.

6. Establish a Key Communicator Network newsletter specifically for these people. After the first year, send out a short evaluation form to see how the network is working and might be improved.

For more information about Key Communicator Networks, contact the National School Public Relations Association, 301.519.0496 and purchase a copy of *A Guidebook for Opinion Leader/Key Communicator Programs*.

Advocacy Tools

Successful advocacy is more than just passion for your vision to improve the rigor of your school. It requires thoughtful development of strategies to share your message and mobilize others to support your vision.

The One-Page Fact Sheet

The one-page fact sheet helps you organize the important facts and points of your issue. It can be used as a handout and it will give you necessary background information, as well as added confidence to discuss the issue. A one-page fact sheet is essential for your preparation. One page is your limit. Most decision-makers want the basic facts and don't want to waste their time. The limit also enables you to keep your message focused.

Key Points in a One-Page Fact Sheet

♦ Clearly define the issue
♦ State your position on the issue
♦ Clarify what you want the decision-maker to do
♦ Define five talking points in order of importance
♦ Provide two references to support issue
♦ Make the sale with a closure statement

Mike Matkovich, a teacher-leader, used this process to develop a one-page fact sheet related to increasing rigor at his high school. With his permission, we adapted it slightly for illustrative purposes.

Sample One-Page Fact Sheet:
Increasing Rigor at XXX High School

Our Goal: To provide students with high quality and high intensity classes in high school for post-secondary success.

Recommendation: Implement a thorough review of all courses and support appropriate revisions to ensure that each of our students are prepared for post-secondary success.

Important Facts:

♦ Most Americans do not believe that schools provide a rigorous enough high school experience.

♦ The fastest growing part of the high school curriculum at the moment is AP classes or college level courses. The fastest growing part of the college curriculum is remedial—or high school classes.

♦ Student readiness for college-level reading is at its lowest point in more than a decade.

♦ The most common misconception about college readiness is that meeting their high school graduation requirements prepares them for college. High schools in states with more demanding graduation standards make more progress in advancing student achievement than schools in states with less rigorous standards.

♦ High school tests address content that does not exceed the 9th or 10th grade.

♦ Improving college readiness is crucial to the development of a diverse and talented labor force that is able to maintain and increase U.S. economic competitiveness throughout the world.

Our Situation:

Less than 30% of our students take advanced courses. Even though 95% of our students pass the exit exam, they are not necessarily prepared for college. Fifteen percent of our students lose their scholarships at the end of their freshman year, due to a low GPA. A recent outside evaluation recommended that we increase rigor in all classes.

Elevator Talk

There are occasions where you have a brief opportunity to make personal contact with a key decision-maker. In those cases, you should be prepared to give a personal story about the importance of your issue—increasing rigor. An elevator talk is a 30-60 second story that includes three elements,

1. Your name and what you do
2. Your key issue
3. What you would like the person to know to do

You should practice telling your story and why you care about this issue with another person. This will give you confidence when you have a golden opportunity: a chance or planned meeting with a stakeholder or "mover and shaker."

Mike also shared with us an elevator talk he planned to use with his superintendent or other district leaders to reinforce the need to improve rigor.

Elevator Talk to Superintendent or District Leader of XXX District

I'm Mike Matkovich, a teacher at the high school in your district. I am very proud of the recognition that our schools have received due to our high test scores and other academic achievements. However, I am concerned that continuing to limit our discussion of rigor to the few Advanced Placement and Honors courses that XXX School District offers, does not meet the demands our students will need to meet in college. Did you know that the fastest growing part of the college curriculum is remedial or basically high school classes? The level of high school courses a student takes has a direct relationship on their success in college, as well as the workplace. Students falter in college because of the large gap between their high school experience and what is expected of them in college. It would do justice not only to our school district, but to the deteriorating economy as well, if our students did not have to retake classes in college they should have mastered in high school. We can do this by offering a more challenging and wide-ranging curriculum that prepares all of our students for the rigors of life after high school.

Having an effective "elevator talk" is essential in networking, engaging partners, and opening new doors. First impressions are easily sabotaged with an elevator talk that's unimpressive because it's too long or too short.

Elevator talks should only be for a one- or two-story building—the time it takes an elevator to traverse one or two floors and no more than 30 seconds. People tire quickly of tedious talk about an issue particularly when part of a casual encounter.

The payoff is the "what's in it for me?" and doesn't always have to be explicitly stated. Potential partners only care about issues of importance to them. You have a maximum of 30 seconds to get them to care. The easiest way to connect quickly is to articulate problems they can identify with. The stated or implied payoff is the solution to those problems.

> **Try This**: Imagine you want to explain to fifth graders the importance of greater rigor in classrooms. Use no jargon or fuzzy words—just simple talk. Now increase the grade level while maintaining the simplicity. Use 20 words or less. Refine and edit your presentation until you have a creative way of conveying your message that stimulates the listener to support your effort.

Advocacy with Parents and Families

Intuitively we know that parents and families are important partners in efforts to improve the rigor of our schools. When families are involved both at home and at school, students do better in school and stay in school longer.

Parents and families can be important allies in improving your school's program. Not only do they support your efforts with their children, they can be advocates for your school with their friends, extended family, and connections throughout the community.

There are three strategies for your advocacy work with families. First, communicate often and with lots of information. Second, provide meaningful roles for parents in school life so that they can see your work to improve rigor. Third, provide support and resources so that they can be successful with their children at home.

Communicate Often You can't communicate too much with families of your students. Be sure to use a variety of media including print as well as electronic alternatives. Many schools have begun to rely on e-mail and other electronic media to communicate with parents. Be cautious about over-relying on this option. In many communities a large number of parents do not have access to the Internet or e-mail at home. By communicating in multiple and varied ways, you can meet the needs of all of your families.

Other ideas for communicating with families include the following:

Communicating with Families

- Publish a family-friendly newsletter on a consistent basis and include information about your efforts to improve rigor
- Identify the need to publish the newsletter and other publications in languages other than English
- Promote personal notes from teachers to families about their children and increasing rigor in their classrooms
- Share information on how families can work with their children to hold them accountable for success at school

---

Occasionally, parents will question a school practice. School leaders must be prepared to talk with parents about the issue and explain how such practices contribute to a culture of increased rigor. Here are some of the most common concerns.

"Not Yet" Grading We know of parents who question a "Not Yet" grading policy. They subscribe to the importance of assigning grades for all student work and identifying those who are most able and those less skilled—winners and losers.

It Doesn't Prepare Them For Real Life We've also heard of parents questioning some practices because "it isn't the way it's done in the 'real' world." The concerns often involve a modified grading policy or a revise and resubmit policy for student work or providing rubrics so that students are clear on expectations.

Do It Right the First Time Similarly some parents question the reasons for providing additional time to complete assignments. They suggest it won't be that way at the next academic level or that it gives children permission to be laggards.

How to Respond

As the school leader you must be able to do more than just support your teachers. You need to know the rationale behind such policies and be able to explain their importance to parents. You need to be able to advocate for such policies and explain the reasons they contribute to increased rigor.

Provide Meaningful Roles in School Families want to be involved with their children's schools. But they want to have meaningful roles and make meaningful contributions.

One of the most important roles is as a member of your School Improvement Team. Family members provide different perspectives and through their involvement can become advocates for your efforts to improve rigor. It is important that you value their input and listen carefully to their point-of-view. One Michigan principal says that parents on his Improvement Team are like an early warning system. "If they don't support the vision or subscribe to our plan, I know others who are less involved won't be supportive."

At Hadley Junior High in Glen Ellyn, IL, parents are members of all planning committees. They participate in all meetings, contribute to the agenda, and both support and challenge school initiatives. But, perhaps most importantly, they know the issues that are important to parents and they have consistently helped craft school communications to other parents and families.

Offer Support and Resources Families also want information that they can use to work with their children at home. Provide families with the resources that can they can use. Recognize that the needs will vary depending on the specific population.

You might want to create a family and community learning center. Identify a place in your school, with adult-sized furnishings; then add basic refreshments and information helpful to parents. You might want to create a library of materials available for parent use. Be careful that materials about your effort to improve rigor avoid the use of educational jargon.

Another alternative is to provide family support groups that deal with topics important to families. You might want to suggest some topics that will help to improve rigor like supporting your child when they do their homework, balancing school work with time to relax and play, or how to select courses in high school that will provide a rigorous experience and strong academic preparation.

Publicize the resources that are available to families. Include information in newsletters and other communications. Keep some of the resources in the main office with a note about others available in the resource center. Be sure that those who need the resources the most know they are available and how to access them.

Talking with Your School Board

Your school board sets district policies and determines the allocation of funds. Because they play a major role in setting district priorities it is important to keep them informed about your school's plans to improve rigor.

Board members are often community leaders who have significant influence with other members of the community. By gathering support from the school board you can build momentum for your plans through the networks and alliance of board members.

- Identify a parent or community spokesperson to help deliver your message to the board;
- Frame the importance of rigor in your opening statement;
- Explain why increased rigor is important;
- Describe your plan;
- Discuss the current state of your plans, giving recognition for successes;
- Provide examples to illustrate the impact. For example, highlight the affect of greater rigor on one or more students; and
- Connect your plans with your vision of greater rigor and emphasize how these plans align and support the board's vision for the district.

Advocacy and the Media

At some point, you will likely be required to deal with the media, whether it is your local newspaper or some form of electronic media. Don't be taken by surprise; anticipate that you will need to communicate with the media and plan appropriately. Preparation is your friend.

You may also want to initiate contact with the media. They can be particularly helpful in sharing information about your school and your work to increase the rigor of your classrooms. Local newspapers are particularly helpful and will often appreciate receiving information about school programs.

Tips for Dealing with the Media

- Preparation is your best friend—learn as much as you can about the reporter, the show, and the audience.
- Establish your communication goals for each interview.
- Determine two or three key points to make to reach your goal.
- Speak in "memorable language."
- Learn and use the "bridging technique." Redirect the interview to your key points.
- Practice, practice, practice. Practice on camera, if possible.

- Do not wear clothes or use mannerisms that distract from your message.
- Forget jargon, now and forever.
- Make sure that the mind is in gear before the mouth travels.
- Look at the reporter when answering questions; turn to the camera when delivering a key point.
- Steady eyes suggest honesty; blinking, darting eyes suggest nervousness and dishonesty.
- Anticipate questions and have answers ready. Once the interview is scheduled, try to figure out what questions the reporter might ask.
- Relax.

Advocacy and Emerging Technology

Traditional media should be part of an advocacy plan but emerging technology can also be helpful to your efforts. You may want to consider ways that "new" technology can help mobilize your community to support your school program.

School Website Use your school's webpage as a way to communicate your vision for a more rigorous school. It can also be a way to share information about meetings and other activities that support your agenda. You may want to make your website, the one-stop spot for information about ways that parents and families can support more rigor in your school.

Social Networking Sites Twitter, Facebook, and other social networking sites have the ability to create a school or organization site. At Twitter, you can "tweet" about upcoming programs and recent successes. Individuals can become a "friend" of a school site on Facebook and have access to updates about the school and its program.

Advocacy Scorecard

Barbara's father is a successful advocate in North Carolina where he provides information about the importance of healthy lifestyles for children and adolescents. We've adapted his work as a tool that principals can use to assess the status of their advocacy efforts.

Final Thoughts

School leaders find themselves working on complex issues in an increasingly complex environment. It is essential that they recognize emerging issues that may impact their school and that they develop the skills to successfully advocate for their schools. This advocacy role requires building networks with groups inside and outside of the educational community, honing a clear message about the importance of increasing rigor in schools, and the confidence to advocate on behalf of their school and its students.

10

Shared Accountability

One of the biggest roadblocks to addressing instructional rigor in schools is the resistance from teachers, students, parents, and other building and district leaders. As we discussed earlier, every person deals differently with change. Some are more accepting, others more resistant.

No change initiative is successful unless shared accountability is established. We suggest that accountability for increasing the rigor of your school's program involves teachers, parents, and students as well as school and district leadership.

Accountability is much more than issuing mandates and expecting compliance. For school leaders it involves energizing and motivating individuals and groups.

The culture of the school must be one where high value is placed on improving students' educational experience, where there is a collective commitment to improvement and a parallel commitment to supporting people who take risks and make changes. Further, the culture must not accept failure as an option. Every student must be expected to learn and the staff must be committed to supporting students in their learning.

Families and community are also integral to school success. School personnel must work with families and community members to ensure that students have the resources to be successful in school and families must be engaged in school life through participation in school governance and responsibility for student success.

Supporting Teachers and Other Staff

Part of the resistance to change is the expectation that people will be held accountable for results. Successful leaders understand that the success of any change initiative is directly related to developing the capacity of the people in the organization to implement the change. The *School Administrators of Iowa*, a professional organization for principals, identified several research-based strategies that principals can use to support people during change (Gold & Roth, 1999). They include the following practices.

Ways to Support Teachers and Staff During Change

- Allow people to discuss feelings of loss and the difficulty of "letting go" of familiar programs and practices;
- Identify the needs of individual people and tailor the support based upon need;
- Develop support groups that are problem solving, action-oriented, and non-judgmental;
- Be candid about unmet needs and work with people to plan specific ways to meet the need;
- Focus on strengths, skills, and interests of each person;
- Provide opportunity for everyone involve to share their ideas and talents;
- Plan ways for individuals to expand their skills to support the innovation;
- Develop personal development plans tailored to each individual involved in implementing the innovation;
- Identify ways that individuals can work to support one another throughout the implementation;
- Focus on successes and achievements;
- Give extra support to those who need it;
- Keep communication open and encouraging

Adapted From: Gold and Roth (1999).

Overcoming Resistance

People respond to change in different ways. Some (5%) are early adopters and eagerly embrace any innovation. Another 5% will never adopt a change; nothing can get them to embrace the innovation. But most people (90%) can be moved toward support if given sufficient time and information.

We've found that people resist change for two primary reasons. They don't see the value of the change or they are not sure they will be as successful with the change. We've found this to be true when working with teachers and principals to improve the rigor of their school.

Some of the most frequent concerns involve changing long-standing practices like grading or classroom organization. We often find intense resistance to the idea of a "Not Yet" grading policy. Teachers may find it cumbersome to implement. Parents may say it doesn't hold students accountable. School leaders may not know how to explain it to parents and community members.

Maslow's hierarchy (1986) is a useful way to think about what happens to people. Under stress related to change people may move to a lower level on the hierarchy. With support they are able to move to higher levels.

Example of Staff Needs	
Aesthetic Need (self-actualization)	Focus on the needs of students first
Need for Understanding Need for Knowledge	What do I need to know to be successful? What opportunities will I have for professional growth? What models exist that can help me plan a more rigorous classroom?
Esteem Needs Belonging Needs	Will I be successful changing my instruction? Will others (colleagues, students, parents) value my work? How do the new norms around rigor align with my beliefs?

Example of Staff Needs (continued)	
Security Needs *Survival Needs*	What will I be teaching? Will I be able to provide a more rigorous educational experience for students? Will I have sufficient materials to provide a rigorous experience for students? Do I have the knowledge and skills for success? Who's making these decisions?

Adapted from: Maslow, 1968; Williamson & Blackburn, 2009.

It's not just teachers who deal with the complexities of change. It also affects students, families, and leaders.

Examples of Stakeholders' Needs			
	Students	*Families*	*Leaders*
Aesthetic (self-actualization)	Focus on own learning first	First priority is supporting child's success	Every action supports success for every student
Need for Understanding *Need for Knowledge*	Will I have the knowledge to be successful? What level of support will I have?	Do I have the information to support my child's success? What examples are available to help me support my child?	Do I have the knowledge and skills to work with teachers, students, and families to improve rigor?

Esteem Needs Belonging Needs	Will I be successful? What will others think of me if I work hard?	Will I be successful changing family habits about homework?	What will other school leaders think of my work on this effort?
Security Needs Survival Needs	What happens if I am unsuccessful? Do I have the knowledge and skills for success?	What happens if my child and I disagree about the importance of school work?	Will my school be successful? Do I have the knowledge and skills to sustain our efforts to improve rigor?

Adapted from: Maslow, 1968; Williamson & Blackburn, 2009.

Have a Clear, Concrete Result

One way to help overcome resistance is to have a clear, concrete result. Teachers and families often need to see a clear, defined outcome. You should always be able to describe what success looks like. For example, "If we are successful implementing _____, we will know it because we will see _____.

You do not need to develop the vision without any input; the most lasting visions are shared ones. However, when working to improve the rigor of your school and classrooms you should be able to provide an explicit, measurable result.

Examples of Clear, Concrete Results

- ◆ Teachers will use more analysis and synthesis questions with students;
- ◆ Students will be able to describe ways that they are supported in their work;
- ◆ Students, teachers, and families can discuss ways that student work samples have changed; and
- ◆ Teachers can explain how classroom routines have been modified to provide time for students to revise and resubmit work.

Building Accountability into Everyday Routines

The most important role of a school leader is supervising the instructional program. But the principal is not the only person responsible for a quality instructional program. Teachers and other staff are responsible for delivering instruction and positively impacting every student's learning.

Principals are, however, responsible for creating a climate and culture at their school that supports quality instruction, rigorous instruction, promotes innovation, and nurtures professional growth.

Ways to Focus Your Culture on Rigor

♦ creating a structure that provides time for collegial discussion and dialogue about increasing rigor;

♦ staying current on educational trends and developments;

♦ accessing professional development and other resources to support more rigorous classrooms;

♦ modeling rigorous instructional practices at meetings and during other interaction with staff; and

♦ attending and actively participating in professional development and other learning opportunities about improving rigor.

Accountability Through Supervisory Practices

Through the supervisory process principals can raise the level of accountability. Glickman, Gordon, and Ross-Gordon (2004) suggest that effective supervision is an ongoing process. It is much more than just evaluating teacher performance. It is all about engaging teachers in reflective conversations about their practice. Effective supervisors understand that teachers are adults and respond well to the principles of adult learning. Effective supervisors are empowering and motivating and provide opportunities for teachers to reflect on and think about their teaching.

Two examples illustrate the importance of these activities. At Crossroads High School in Georgia the principal and others conduct weekly instructional walkthroughs. While not unusual, the emphasis on observing rigor in the classroom is unique. If rigor is not observed, at the end of the third walkthrough the principal schedules a time to talk with the teacher and identify steps to improve rigor.

We've developed an example of a walkthrough protocol that can be used to measure progress on increasing rigor. A portion of the protocol is provided here.

Rigorous Schools and Classrooms Walkthrough

This protocol is used to gather data about the school's progress implementing the rigorous schools and classrooms indicators. It is not designed to be part of personnel evaluation. The protocol is useful in identifying school-wide trends and issues.

Indicator	Notes & Questions
Learner-centered Instruction ♦ Teachers maintain high expectations for all students. ♦ Support and scaffolding are provided to ensure success. ♦ There is evidence of student high-order thinking. ♦ Students are active in all aspects of learning. ♦ Lessons incorporate application activities seamlessly.	*Expectations for Learning* ♦ Teachers are consistent in the belief that students can learn, will learn, and that they have the power to help them do so. ♦ Lessons are designed so students see the value of specific learning. ♦ Teachers are persistent in supporting student learning. ♦ Interaction with students reflects the belief that it is unacceptable to not learn.

The principal of Chapin Middle School in Chapin, SC uses a weekly newsletter to highlight information about rigor and examples that have been observed throughout the school.

In *The Principalship from A to Z* we describe a model for effective supervision. Centered on improving teacher instruction, it includes a pre-conference and a post-observation conference. We've found that the best instructional conferences provide ample opportunity for the teacher to process and reflect on his or her own practice.

Almost all school districts have an established evaluation process including established timelines and forms. We recognize the legal requirements to follow those guidelines but also want to suggest a protocol for classroom observations related to rigor.

Central to our protocol is the recognition that every characteristic of a rigorous classroom will not be present in each lesson. We believe what is important is the pattern that develops over multiple classroom visits.

Here is a portion of a classroom observation form that could be used when visiting classrooms.

Classroom Observation Form	
Teacher:	Date:
Grade/Subject:	
Instructions: Rate each item on a scale from 1 to 5 with 1 indicating low implementation and 5 indicating high implementation. Provide evidence gathered during the classroom observation to support the rating.	

The teacher . . .	*Rating and Evidence Observed*
1. Acts consistently on the unwavering belief that each student can and will learn, and on the teacher's power to help them do so.	Rating: Evidence:
2. Regularly provides support and scaffolding needed to ensure each student's success.	Rating: Evidence:
3. Provides support that is customized so that students are not allowed not to learn.	Rating: Evidence:

This is only a sample and not a complete observation form. We think the very best data is collected over multiple observations rather than relying on a single observation.

Some of the most productive conversations about rigor occur following the classroom observation. Teachers value the time to think about their work and reflect on its success.

The process of reflection is a critical part of implementing an instructional innovation. Often the most skilled teachers are most interested in an opportunity to reflect on their teaching and consider ways to grow professionally.

The most useful prompts are open-ended. They do not lend themselves to a single answer and are designed to promote teacher reflection. The discussion cannot be seen as evaluative nor punitive. It must be supportive and encourage professional growth.

Suggested Post-Observation Discussion Prompts

- Thank you for the opportunity to visit your classroom. I would like to have you talk with me about the lesson.
- When you plan a lesson, what things do you consider? How do you plan to address our goal of improved rigor for students?
- Describe ways that you monitor student learning during your lessons? What clues do you gather about student learning?
- As you continue to implement—what do you consider the appropriate next steps?
- What additional support or resources may I provide for you? How can I support your effort to improve the rigor in your classroom?

Accountability Through Professional Development

Professional development is an essential tool for realizing your vision of a more rigorous school. As discussed in Chapter Eight, you need to have a clear purpose linked to research and data about student needs.

You must also assure accountability for the use of professional development in classrooms. We believe that one of the most effective means to accountability is that of one person to another. At one school where Ron worked teachers were responsible for sharing one new idea they implemented at the first staff meeting after any professional development activity. They met in small groups, shared their ideas and asked for suggestions and feedback from colleagues. This shared accountability led to greater use of the innovations.

There are other ways that you can assure accountability for the use of professional development. They include an instructional walkthrough organized and led by teachers, opportunity to examine student work samples, or lesson study activities. You might also ask for samples of student work rather than request to see lesson plans.

Accountability Through School Improvement

Too often school improvement is not linked to the school's vision. It is driven by either local or state mandates to have a School Improvement Plan.

We suggest that you use your school improvement process to support your vision of a more rigorous school.

In one school district outside of Detroit Ron led a project to improve the rigor of the middle school program. After developing a shared vision about rigor, the group examined data about student learning, student demographics, and teacher and student perceptions about the learning environment. These data guided decisions about organizing the instructional day.

Most importantly, the group agreed on a set of indicators, or data points, that would be routinely monitored by the School Improvement Team in each school. They committed to using that data to guide decisions about both short-term and long-term school improvement goals.

Accountability Through Work with Families and Community

It is also important that your vision for a more rigorous school be regularly shared with families and with members of your community. In Chapter Nine we suggested that you develop a set of talking points that you can use to build support for your vision. It is also important to provide families with the information and tools they need to support your vision of a more rigorous school.

It is important to be proactive rather than reactive when talking with stakeholder groups. One principal in suburban Phoenix asked his staff to share "turnaround" stories with him—stories of students who made a significant positive change in their learning. He always had two or three different stories that he could share with families, in formal and informal conversation about the school.

When Barbara went to a curriculum night Apple Valley Middle School in Fletcher, NC, she immediately noticed the school's core belief—learning is not optional. That message was shared with families and re-enforced throughout the evening's activities.

We've found that families are almost always supportive of increasing the quality and rigor of their child's school. Often, however, they want specific ideas about how they can be helpful. Here is a list of ideas we've learned from our work with teachers and principals.

Sample Ideas for Supporting Parents

♦ Provide tips for how to organize the home to support completing homework;

♦ Help families locate libraries and other helpful resources;

♦ Organize parent support groups;

♦ Create a parent library with books and materials about parenting and children's academic growth;

♦ Include tips for parents in every school newsletter;

♦ Arrange for parents to share ideas and strategies for supporting their child's success in school;

These efforts help re-enforce your agenda for a more rigorous school and provide families and community with tangible results of your efforts.

Possible Talking Points

♦ Current data about student learning (test scores, major projects, and assignments)

♦ Awards and recognitions received by students and staff

♦ Examples of students who made a positive change in their learning

♦ Teachers who did "whatever it takes" to ensure student success

---

In Hall County, GA, there is a commitment to rigor for all students. The Hall County Schools have an Assistant Director of Teaching and Learning with responsibility for rigor. Their commitment to rigor is evident on their website http://www.hallco.org/rigor.

We want to thank Dr. Sally Krisel, Assistant Director of Teaching and Learning, for allowing us to share a letter they use to let parents know about their vision of rigor for all. It is a good example of how to advocate with families about your vision for improved rigor.

Dear Parents,

On our web page, in other publications, and in our daily work here in Hall County Schools, we are focused on the motto *"Character, Competency, and Rigor . . . for All."* But what do we mean by the term "rigor"?

Essentially, we believe that mastery of challenging and meaningful content must be our goal for *all* students. Whether they are performing at, below, or above the levels of their age peers, all students deserve an education that challenges them just above their current levels of development. I believe that every student should come to school every day thinking, *"Wow, this class is tough! But I know my teacher will help me, and I know that if I work hard, I can do it!"*

We must ask all students, including those who can quite easily achieve "adequate" indicators of achievement by No Child Left Behind (NCLB) standards, to stretch, to achieve at levels commensurate with their peers, not just nationally but internationally! There is great power in high expectations, and I believe that all our young people can do far more than we have typically asked them to do. Taking this proficiency view of students, i.e., focusing on their strengths and interests as we increase the level of academic challenge, is the best way to change the culture of schools. Simply put, adequacy is not enough for our children; we must have excellence!

I would also like to clarify what we believe rigor is NOT. It is not just asking our children to do more of the same (*"Complete all the problems on page 30 . . . PLUS the bonus problems."*). Yes, we want our children to be engaged in curriculum that pushes them, but not in a joyless, repetitive sense. As I work with teachers on ways to raise the academic bar, we are also talking about ways to make curriculum more meaningful and interesting for students. In summary, we are asking teachers to improve the "authenticity" of the work they ask students to do. Using the language of Dr. Fred Newmann's work on *Authentic Intellectual Work,* we are focusing on the following:

♦ **Construction of Knowledge**—We want students to *use* what they learn, not just repeat it. Students should be asked to grapple with information and ideas by synthesizing, generalizing, explaining, and drawing conclusions that produce new understandings for them—just the things that we as adults do in the world of work!

♦ **Disciplined Inquiry**—Instruction must focus on important concepts within the discipline, and students should learn them with such thoroughness that they are capable of exploring connections and relationships so they have a deeper understanding of the subject. Also, students should be able to discuss subject matter in depth with their classmates and their teachers in ways that build improved understanding.

♦ **Value Beyond School**—Rigorous curriculum should have clear connections to students' lives. We want our teachers helping students see the connections between substantive knowledge and either public problems or personal experiences in their lives outside of school.

Commitment to rigorous curriculum means that we envision each learner on an "escalator of development" and envision ourselves—teachers and parents working together—as seeing to it that each escalator moves steadily upward in all those areas required for persistent intellectual, emotional, and moral growth in all students. Here on the Rigor web page, we put the spotlight on some of the best examples of rigorous learning opportunities . . . and the extraordinary way Hall County students are responding!

Dr. Sally Krisel
Assistant Director of Teaching and Learning (Academic Rigor)

Reprinted with permission of the Hall County Schools.

Accountability for Students

Students also share accountability for their own learning. They are often not included in efforts to increase rigor.

We believe students must be actively involved in their own learning, by making decision about their learning and by being responsible for asking questions, being clear about their work and completing assignments.

Students must also know the expectations for their work. Some of their most frequent questions include: What are the grading standards? Where do I go for additional support? How do I locate examples of a high quality assignment? Where may I locate resources to complete my work?

We recently learned of a program at East Fairmont Junior High School in Fairmont, WV. It is called "Failure is Not an Option" and built on the belief that student behaviors will not change until adult behaviors change. Christine Miller, Principal, shared the details of their program. It is designed to help learns understand their responsibility to complete work in a timely manner. They accept no excuses about failure to complete. Teachers handle all missing assignment up to three. After that, the office is informed and the student must report to the office to complete their work and failure results in removal from the regular lunchroom. Parents then get informed of the failure.

The "Failure is Not an Option" program is a good example of changing practices to let students know about the commitment to their learning and success.

As we discussed in Chapter Two, the evidence is clear that students thrive in an environment when they are expected to complete rigorous and challenging tasks as long as they are provided clear directions, multiple opportunities to demonstrate their learning, and high levels of support.

Focus and Refocus the Conversation

It is very easy to become distracted by personal agendas. All too frequently we've heard issues portrayed as impacting students when in fact it was an issue affecting a teacher or group of teachers.

At a recent workshop about developing a remediation plan for at-risk students two teachers began to argue about classroom space and their own scheduling needs. The two continued to bicker for some time until the principal reminded everyone that the purpose of the remediation classes was to positively affect student learning for their neediest students. By reframing the conversation, the group was able to move beyond the personal agenda.

It is important to always keep your vision about change and about how to improve rigor in your school at the forefront of any conversation. Pulling the conversation back to an agreed upon vision is one way to refocus the conversation.

A strategy that Ron uses when he works with schools on planning projects is to begin every meeting with an opportunity to review their vision. He includes the vision in the PowerPoint he uses and makes it one of the first things each group does. Ron asks each group to, "Take a minute and read the vision statement. Think about how that statement can guide our work today."

Leadership in Action

Dan Ingham, Principal of John Glenn High School in the Wayne-Westland (MI) Schools has worked with his staff to implement significant changes in their school. Dan developed a set of his "Ten Commitments" that would guide his work with his staff. We think they provide a model for how other leaders can focus their work on increasing the rigor of their school.

The Ten Commitments

1. Remain Focused on Learning for All: Consistently model the passion and persistence of our primary purpose—to help all students learn at high levels.
2. Develop and Sustain the School Structure and Culture as a Professional Learning Community (PLC): A PLC defined as, educators working in effective, high-performing collaborative teams, working interdependently, focused on collective inquiry, action research, and data driven best practices to achieve better results for students.
3. Organize into Collaborative Culture: School will function as collaborative teams of professionals who work together interdependently to develop common pacing, design common assessments, and achieve common goals for which members are mutually accountable.
4. Provide for Job-Embedded Professional Development and Adult Learning: Raise student achievement by embedding ongoing and continuous professional development in the routine work of every educator.
5. Empower and Support Teacher Leadership: Develop the capacity of teachers throughout the school to assume leadership roles and view herself or himself as a learning leader of leaders. Tap into everyone's "islands of excellence."
6. Stay Fixated on the Evidence of Learning: Every educator and every team will be expected to use results to inform and impact their professional practice, guide the process of continuous improvement, and facilitate continuous adult and student learning.

7. Implement a Balance of Summative and Formative Assessments: Use a balanced variety of assessments as a powerful tool for improving the teaching and learning process.

8. Assure a Systematic Response When Students Don't Learn: Ensure students who are not learning receive extra time and support that is. timely, directive, and systematic. Create a system of tiered interventions of increasing intensity for students who struggle.

9. Enrich and Extend Learning for Students Already Proficient: Challenge and stretch all students by raising the academic bar. Ensure students of all abilities have clear opportunities for extra time and support and all students will benefit.

10. Celebrate, Celebrate, Celebrate: Publicly celebrate all improvements in behavior and results that will nourish the change effort. Emotionally reward hard workers and build momentum. Win small. Win early. Win often.

From: Ingham, 2008.

It Starts and Ends with Me

During the last decade there has been a significant shift in accountability in schools. School staff share a collective accountability for the success of their students and every individual shares a personal responsibility and accountability for doing whatever it takes to ensure student success.

Ultimately it all starts and ends with each individual's personal vision for their school or classroom, their commitment to making the changes to ensure greater rigor, and their willingness to take risks, support one another, work collaboratively, and abandon long-standing practices that are not successful.

Our individual commitment to be held accountable for the success of our schools, our classrooms, and our students is what will make the biggest difference for students.

Final Thoughts

Improving the rigor of your school is a shared responsibility requiring shared accountability. It is important to support teachers and other staff when implementing your vision for increased rigor, individually and as a group. The focus must remain on continuous improvement rather than compliance with established mandates.

11

Structures to Support Rigor

The way your school is organized can impact your ability to become more rigorous. Structure can be either a barrier to reform or a way to accelerate the work. This chapter will examine ways that structure can be used to support a shared vision for creating a more rigorous school.

Throughout the chapter we will discuss structures that support teachers, students, families, and leaders as they work to improve the rigor of their school. We will include ways to organize teachers and students for instruction, suggest several different ways to provide time for collaboration on improving rigor, and include examples from schools around the country.

Professional Learning Communities

Creating a professional learning community (PLC) is common in many schools. It is one way to think about working collaboratively to improve the rigor of your school and your classrooms. PLC's take many forms but are almost uniformly focused on improving student learning. Chapter Eight: Professional Development provides a detailed description of professional learning communities and the way they can accelerate your efforts to improve rigor.

Central to the vitality of a professional learning community is a value on collaborative activity and a recognition that teachers and other personnel must be provided with time to meet, talk about rigor in your school, and identify strategies for making your school more rigorous. The focus is on continuous improvement with a results orientation. One principal described it as a "laser light focus on getting the desired results."

Characteristics of Successful Professional Learning Communities
♦ Continuous program improvement ♦ Rigorous, relevant curriculum and instruction ♦ Interdisciplinary teaching and instructional teams

Adapted from: Oxley, D., Barton, R. & Klump, J. (2006). Creating small learning communities. *Principal's Research Review, 1*(6), p. 3.

Time for Collaboration

It is important that teachers have time to work with colleagues on professional tasks. This collaborative time is one of the catalysts for nurturing and sustaining change. Teachers value the opportunity to meet with grade or content peers to discuss successes, diagnose ways to improve, and develop a repertoire of strategies that they can use in their own classrooms.

There are many different ways to provide collaborative time. They vary considerably depending on the grade level of the school.

Ways to Provide Collaborative Time	
Common Planning	When teachers share a common planning period some of the time may be used for collaborative work.
Parallel Scheduling	When special teachers (physical education, music, art, etc.) are scheduled so that grade level or content area teachers have common planning.

Shared Classes	Teachers in more than one grade or team combine their students into a single large class for specific instruction and the other teachers can collaborate.
Faculty Meeting	Find other ways to communicate the routine items shared during faculty meetings and reallocate that time to collaborative activities.
Adjust Start or End of Day	Members of a team, grade, or entire school agree to start their workday early or extend their workday one day a week to gain collaborative time.
Late Start or Early Release	Adjust the start or end of the school day for students and use the time for collaborative activity.
Professional Development Days	Rather than traditional large group professional development use the time for teams of teachers to engage in collaborative work.

Adapted from: Williamson, 2009; DuFour, DuFour, Eaker & Many, 2006.

Angela Evans, the Instructional Dean at Tulsa Technology Center shared how her school provides collaborative time. They developed a "released time" schedule that allows every teacher to work with other teachers on instructional issues. The deans organize the schedule to provide two days for this important work.

Regardless of the way you provide time for collaboration, the most important thing is how you use the time. It is important that it be productive and supports your vision of improved rigor.

Sample Tasks

- ♦ meet in vertical teams to work on articulation of the curriculum
- ♦ work with grade level teachers to examine student work
- ♦ talk with the School Improvement Team about conducting walk-throughs focused on rigor
- ♦ Conduct a book study on *Rigor is Not a Four-Letter Word*

Organizing to Provide Collaborative Time

Many schools change their schedule to provide additional collaborative time. There are many different ways to organize the schedule (Williamson, 2009) but some provide more opportunity for collaboration than others.

Here are some of the ways we've found most effective at providing time for teachers to collaborate. We've grouped them into elementary and secondary examples but many of the strategies work in both settings.

Elementary School Examples

Location of Classrooms

Most elementary schools are organized into self-contained classrooms, particularly in the early grades. A common way to promote collaboration is to locate all early elementary classes on the same floor or in the same wing. Similarly, all the later elementary classes can be located near one another. One principal we met said that it "allowed each wing to focus on the developmental issues with their students" and "promoted collaboration among grade-level teachers."

Other schools we've visited place a class or two from each grade in a wing of the building. This organization is designed to provide interaction among the grades and ease the grouping and regrouping for instruction.

Of course, just locating classrooms near one another does not guarantee collaboration. It just provides the opportunity to collaborate.

Scheduling Special Classes

One way to provide collaborative time for teachers is to schedule special classes such as music, art, and physical education so that teachers at a single grade or combination of grades have common planning.

Many elementary teachers want an extended block of time in the morning for literacy and mathematics instruction. Since all special classes cannot be scheduled in the afternoon it is important to talk with your teachers about how you might arrange for collaborative time.

Parallel Schedule

Many elementary schools organize classrooms to provide greater content-specific instruction. At each grade level one or two teachers might specialize in math and science and one or two others specialize in reading, language arts, and social studies.

By organizing all the teachers at a grade level so that they have a similar schedule, including when students go to special classes, you create time each day when those teachers can meet and collaborate. This time can be used to discuss instruction, develop common assessments, look at student work, or diagnose student learning needs.

	1	*2*	*3*	*4*	*5*
Teacher A	Reading/LA	Reading/LA	S P E C I A L S	Reading/LA	Reading/LA
Teacher B	Reading/LA	Reading/LA		Reading/LA	Reading/LA
Teacher C	Math/Sci	Math/Sci		Math/Sci	Math/Sci
Teacher D	Math/Sci	Math/Sci		Math/Sci	Math/Sci

Secondary School Examples

Teaming

More than half of the middle schools and many high schools organize students and teachers into instructional teams. Teams consist of a group of teachers who share students and often have common planning time to meet and talk about curricular and instructional issues.

Teaming has been shown to have a positive impact on student learning and school climate when teams meet and spend most of their common planning time working on ways to improve student learning. We've found that the most effective teams are committed to talking about their instruction, about ways to increase the rigor of their classrooms, and about ways to provide additional support for student learning.

School-Within-A-School

One way to respond to the anonymity present in large schools is to organize into smaller units, often called houses or small schools-within-a-school. In such a model students and teachers often remain in the same unit for most of the day.

Teachers in a school-within-a-school model often have common planning and a time to work collaborative on instructional improvement.

Organization of Curricular Departments

Another strategy for promoting collaboration among teachers is to group curricular departments together rather than maintaining a separate organization. At New Trier High School, Northfield Campus, outside of Chicago, principal Jan Borga put math and science teachers together into the same department. They shared office space and were expected to work collaboratively on curriculum design, interdisciplinary links, and instructional improvement. Her goal was to ensure a more rigorous academic experience for students, one that maximized support and opportunity for learning. A similar arrangement impacted other curricular areas.

Common Planning for Content Teachers

Yet another way to promote collaboration is to arrange the schedule so that teachers of a single course, or combination of courses, share a planning period. Richard Barajas, principal of Milby High School in Houston, TX, organized the schedule of his Algebra teachers this way.

With common planning the Algebra teachers were expected to meet with one of the school's curricular specialists to design common assessments. Teachers were expected to teach the curriculum, use the assessments, and be prepared to discuss student success with the assessments. The discussions focused on what teachers learned about "what worked and what didn't work" in their lessons. They provided an opportunity to work collaboratively to redesign lessons that were less effective than desired and to reinforce practices that contributed to student success.

Your School's Schedule as a Tool to Increase Rigor

Managing the school's schedule can be one of the most complex and time-consuming tasks faced by school leaders. Often the focus is on the logistics of the schedule but we've found that the most successful schools see the schedule as a tool that can be used to positively impact their instructional program.

Through the schedule you can provide time for teachers to work together on strategies to improve rigor. They can create varied instructional designs, provide additional support for students, and offer more in-depth instruction.

Your school's schedule is a powerful tool to improve rigor and provide teachers with the tools they need to implement your shared vision of a more rigorous school.

> **Principles About School Schedules**
>
> ◆ Schedules reflect a school's values and priorities
> ◆ The most effective schedules are anchored in a shared vision
> ◆ A quality schedule emerges when teachers and administrators work together in establishing priorities and selecting a design
> ◆ Without clear goals, the schedule is merely a plan for organizing teachers and students; when guided by goals, the schedule becomes a powerful tool to positively impact teaching and learning

From: Williamson & Blackburn (2009).

The first step is to talk with key stakeholders about the schedule. A shared vision and clarity of purpose helps build support for the schedule. For example, you might want to talk with your School Improvement Team about the schedule and how it might support your vision of a rigorous school.

Organize the conversation around a series of questions designed to promote thinking and generate ideas. The staff at Bay Village Middle School in northern Ohio worked with Ron on just this issue. They organized their thinking around these three questions:

◆ How do we allocate time to content areas based on student need?
◆ What are several ways that we can create longer instructional blocks and provide regular time for teacher's to collaborate?
◆ How do we provide flexibility so that students who need extra time or support have that option?

The questions served to organize their thinking and kept the discussion focused.

Value collaboration. We've found that building support among those responsible for implementing any initiative is important. Talk openly about every option. Discuss advantages and disadvantages. Communicate with stakeholders and provide an opportunity for them to provide suggestions and input. Chapter Six: Ownership and Shared Vision offers suggestions for ways to promote collaboration. Chapter Nine: Advocacy provides ideas about communicating with stakeholders.

Schedules that Support a Rigorous School

There are many different kinds of schedules. All have advantages and disadvantages and reflect values about the use of time, opportunity for collaboration, and the importance of providing additional support for students.

We've identified several scheduling approaches that can positively impact the rigor of your school. We want to be very clear, however. The schedule is just a tool that creates a structure to improve rigor. The key is how the time is used. It cannot be used merely to increase coverage. Here are some questions you might want to use as you think about changing your schedule.

♦ How will it provide greater depth in the curriculum?
♦ How will it increase rigor in instructional activities?
♦ How will it increase the opportunities for support for students?

Block Schedules

Block schedules provide long instructional blocks that teachers can use for greater instructional flexibility. Block schedules often release energy and creativity among teachers when they know they are not bound by a fixed period schedule.

Middle schools that organize into instructional teams often assign every teacher on a team a similar schedule. They also get common planning time. Teachers can reorganize their block into longer instructional periods to support instructional needs.

Examples of activities possible with a longer block include regrouping for large or small-group instruction, laboratory-type activities, team meetings, interdisciplinary or thematic units, learning activities that involve creating, building or making a product, or additional support for student learning.

	Fixed Period Schedule	*Block Schedule*
1	Mathematics	Team decides on time given to each content area
2	Science	
3	Language Arts	
4	Social Studies	
5	Elective/Exploratory	Elective/Exploratory
6	Elective/Exploratory	Elective/Exploratory

Many high schools have also adopted a block schedule commonly called a four-by-four block. In such a schedule each class is longer and fewer classes meet each day. At some schools the classes alternate from day to day. At others the classes meet daily and change at the end of the semester.

	Semester 1	*Semester 2*
1	Geometry	Concert Band
2	English 10	World History
3	Economics	Spanish 2
4	Physical Education	Biology

The four-by-four block schedule allows teachers to design lessons with opportunity for more in-depth instruction, time for guided practice, and more time to monitor student learning.

Alternating Day Schedules

An additional scheduling tool is to alternate classes so that they do not meet every day. Alternating schedules may provide longer blocks of time for classes and are often used to provide an opportunity for students to take additional classes. Some schools use the alternating day schedule as a way to provide time for additional instruction or other supports for students. Below is an example of an alternating schedule.

Mon	*Tue*	*Wed*	*Thu*	*Fri*
English	Spanish	English	Spanish	English
Math	Chemistry	Math	Chemistry	Math
Phys Ed.	US History	Phys Ed.	US History	Phys Ed.
Band	Drama	Band	Drama	Band

This example shows the schedule for one week. The next week the schedule would be reversed with the four classes meeting on Tuesday and Thursday meeting on Monday, Wednesday, and Friday.

Another example of an alternating day schedule builds in an every other day student support period. This support period is scheduled at the same time for every student. Students have time to access the testing center, meet with their counselor, work on longer assignments, meet with teachers, or conduct research for completing assignments.

Mon	*Tue*	*Wed*	*Thu*	*Fri*
Geometry	Orchestra	Geometry	Spanish	Geometry
French	Economics	French	Economics	French
Biology	**Support**	Biology	**Support**	Biology
Phys Ed.	English	Phys Ed.	Drama	Phys Ed.

Trimester Schedules

Yet another approach to organizing the school day is to use a trimester model. The school year is divided into three equal parts, with courses scheduled accordingly.

The ability for a student who fails a class to "recover" more quickly is one of the major advantages of a trimester model. In a traditional schedule a student might need to wait a full year before being able to retake a class. With the trimester model the student can repeat the class more quickly, the next trimester.

Some classes may meet one trimester, some two, and some even all three trimesters. Generally each class period is longer than in a traditional schedule and most classes meet only one trimester.

	Fall	*Winter*	*Spring*
1	Algebra 1	Biology	English 1B

2	English 1A	US History	Spanish 1B
3	Phys Ed.	Spanish 1A	Spanish 1B
4	Band	Band	Band

Structures for Extra Support

Our definition of rigor (Chapter Three) includes the importance of expecting students to learn at high levels and supporting students so that they can learn. Structures to support students are essential to becoming a more rigorous school.

Teachers and school leaders have told us about the importance of motivating students to do well in school and supporting their success. Here are three examples we find useful.

Example 1: Student Rewards Program

Keith Rydell, Principal of the Vantage Career Center in Van Wert, OH, provided one example of a student rewards program.

> The program is called GOALS and students earn points in each category and are treated to a reward each quarter if they earn sufficient points.
>
> G = good grades
> O = good organization
> A = good attendance
> L = strong leadership
> S = strong academic skills and service

Example 2: Student Recognition Program

Beth Hill, Assistant Principal at Doss High School in the Louisville, KY, shares an alternate way to recognize students.

> Students can receive a "Caught being COOL" card from administrators during observations and walkthroughs. Half the card is a homework pass. The other half gets turned in for a weekly raffle.
>
> C—Conscientious
> O—On-Task
> O—Outstanding
> L—Learner

Example 3: Academic Success Time

A third option comes from Courtney Paul from Raymore-Peculiar Middle School in Missouri.

> We created *Academic Success Time* during the school day to assist students who may be struggling in a subject area. It is like tutoring during school and allows us to get to the students who might not participate in after school tutoring.

Motivating Unmotivated Students

We're told repeatedly about students who come to class with few materials, no books, and a lackluster attitude. In her book on *Classroom Motivation from A to Z* (2005) Barbara provides many examples of ways to motivate students and engage them in learning. Here are several important things about motivation.

First, every student is motivated by two things—value and success. Value is whether the person sees value in what they are doing. Success is whether or not they believe they will be successful and feel successful.

Value Find ways to link what student are learning to things in their own lives and to things they find useful. Barbara once saw a teacher teach a math lesson about positive and negative integers. Students said they would never use a number line but the teacher illustrated the lesson with examples ranging from using money to the yards gained or lost in a football game. It is important to look at the content through the students' eyes.

Success Every one of us is motivated by success. Too often our students have not experienced success and have learned to become disengaged. It's just not enough for the teacher to tell students they can be successful. They must experience success. So, it is important to design lessons and assignments where students can be successful. It is not about "softball" lessons that expect little from students. It is about rigorous expectations but doing things to make the task manageable. For example, divide rigorous projects into smaller pieces so that students can figure out where to start. We need to support students and allow them to experience success so that they can build on that experience in other settings.

Getting Extra Help and Support

There are many great ideas for providing extra help and support to student. Barry Knight, Principal of Palmetto Middle School in Anderson, SC, worked with his faculty to develop several different ways to provide extra help and motivate students to complete their work. We enjoyed his ideas so much we want to share some of them with you.

Extra Help and Support

IMAX—Initiative to Maximize Academic Excellence—A school-wide approach to keeping learning going and to help students succeed who are comfortable with failure. At the end of each month (exact date a secret) students with no Incompletes are awarded a treat for their diligence in completing schoolwork (ice cream, music, fruit, free time, coupons to school store, tickets to events). Students with Incompletes remain with their academic teachers to finish their work.

Lunch Time Learning—A center that is open every day during lunch to provide academic support to students.

LIFT (Letting Individuals Fine-Tune)—Each Wednesday during related arts classes students who need additional instruction to reach mastery are required to meet with their academic teachers for additional small group instruction.

Rock'n RAP—Teachers assist students with research work and encourage reading newspapers and magazines with music, creating an inviting atmosphere.

21st Century Learning Center—Provides healthy snacks, supervised recreational activity, homework assistance, and special learning programs for students after school. Bus transportation is provided.

Leadership in Action

A couple of years ago Ron worked with the Walled Lake Public Schools (MI) to identify ways that they could provide additional collaborative time for their high school teachers. He worked with a group of teachers and administrations representing all curricular areas and each of the high schools.

After first identifying their goals and priorities, the group developed several prototype schedules. Following an analysis of the advantages and disadvantages of each they recommended a model that created two blocks each week for a "seminar" period. The "seminar" was designed to provide time for students to get additional instruction from teachers, to revise and resubmit assignments, and to support those students who needed additional time to complete assignments. Of course, the seminar also provided opportunity for some students to gain more in-depth knowledge in an area of interest.

To find the time for two "seminar" periods the daily schedule was modified. Formerly the high schools had a traditional seven-period day. Under the revised schedule, the day was constructed around six longer class periods (30 per week). Each class met just four times per week (28 total). The two remaining class periods were used for "seminar."

Monday	Tuesday	Wednesday	Thursday	Friday
1	7	5	4	2
2	Seminar	6	5	3
3	1	7	6	4
4	2	1	7	5
5	3	2	Seminar	6
6	4	3	1	7

Structures to Support Families

Families are also partners in your vision of a more rigorous school. It is important to provide them with the knowledge and tools about how they can support the school's work and their child's success.

We described some structures that support parents in Chapters Nine and Ten. Chapter Nine provided a set of ideas about how to provide parents with the knowledge about your school and ways to mobilize their support for your vision of a more rigorous school. Chapter Ten discussed accountability and provided a set of strategies to engage parents in your work to increase rigor.

We've found the following structures helpful to families.

Ways to Support Families

♦ Provide frequent communication, using multiple methods, about your school's vision of increased rigor;

♦ Create a website where parents can access resources about family activities that support success in school (meals, sleep, quiet time for homework, place to do homework);

♦ Organize a forum where families can share ideas about how they support student success; and

♦ Arrange workshops for parents on topics that will support your agenda of increased rigor.

Structures to Support the Leader

It is also important to consider structures that will support you as a leader. Often leaders neglect their own need for support and continued learning.

We've learned that it is essential for leaders to have time to reflect on their own work, process their own learning, and consider how they can refine what they are doing to improve the rigor of their school.

We encourage you to consider some of the following ideas.

Ways to Support Yourself as a Leader

♦ Identify a coach or mentor who you can talk with about your work. Good coaches enable leaders to process their learning and to step back and reflect on how they might improve their work.

♦ Stay current in the field by reading voraciously, attending conferences, and other professional development activities.

♦ Find time to meet with colleagues to share ideas and think about how you can support one another's efforts.

♦ Join your professional association and access its newsletters, journals, and other materials.

Final Thoughts

The organization and structure of your school is one of your most powerful tools for shaping your school's program. It is critical to recognize the connection between the structure—the way you use time, arrangements for collaboration, opportunity for sustained discussion of student learning—and improving the rigor of your school.

12

Challenges and Opportunities

Even with the best planning and supportive implementation you will experience challenges to achieving your vision for a more rigorous school.

We've identified some challenges that emerge most frequently. First, is deciding where to begin. You might be feeling a little overwhelmed. It would be great if you could just snap your fingers and things would be different. But, that's not the way it works.

The reality is that creating a more rigorous school is not easy. It takes time, effort, and persistence. If you have not already done so, there are several things that must be done before you develop a plan.

First, you must work with teachers and other stakeholders to develop a shared vision for a rigorous school. A shared vision is the foundation for all of your efforts. That's why we asked you at the end of Chapter One to write your own vision. It starts with your personal vision of a rigorous school. Take a moment to review what you wrote. How would you like to revise it?

Second, you need to select a starting point. The most successful schools gather data about their current status and use that data to identify their next steps. Use the data to guide development of an action plan.

Now that you've learned about the COMPASS model for improving rigor we'd encourage you to think about two or three ideas that you find particularly interesting or relevant to your vision and situation—things you'd like to try.

Top Three Ideas to Consider	*Ideas I'd Like to Try Later*

As you consider your current situation, you may be thinking, "This is great, but there are going to be problems as I try to increase rigor." There are always obstacles to progress. Let's look at several.

Challenges to Increasing Rigor

◆ Resistance from Stakeholders
◆ Grading
◆ Stable or Declining Resources
◆ Turnover in Leadership

Resistance from Stakeholders

One of the biggest challenges you will face is the resistance that emerges from teachers, students, and families. There are four tools that can help you deal with resistance.

> ### *Tools for Dealing with Resistance*
> - ♦ Understand the resistance
> - ♦ Check your own commitment
> - ♦ Work to change attitudes
> - ♦ Focus conversation on students

Understand the Resistance

Not everyone who resists increasing rigor does so because of ulterior motives. Often there is a conflict between their personal beliefs and values and the proposed changes. For example, in Michigan many educators and parents opposed the idea of increasing the mathematics requirement for high school graduation. A survey found that many of those resisting the idea were concerned that the new requirement would increase dropouts. Their motives were anchored in concern for students, not outright resistance to an idea. As the new requirements were implemented much of the resistance faded when students were provided additional academic support, multiple opportunities to succeed, and different instructional approaches.

While some people resist just to resist, most don't. They are genuinely concerned about the proposed change. They either don't see the value in the change or they have concerns about how successful the change will be.

The Southwest Educational Development Lab developed a way of monitoring change efforts. The Concerns-Based Adoption Model (CBAM) (Hord, Rutherford, Huling-Austin & Hall, 1987) helps you understand what occurs when a school moves from implementing a change, like increasing rigor, to institutionalizing that change.

They created the CBAM model and identified seven stages of concern. It recognizes that change is complex and people experience changes individually from minimal awareness of the innovation to identifying ways to improve on the innovation.

Stages of Concern	Examples of Expression of Concern
6 Refocusing	What else can we do to improve rigor? How can I make my classroom even more rigorous?
5 Collaboration	I'm pleased with my effort to improve rigor, but I wonder what others have done?
4 Consequence	Now that I've increased rigor, how am I doing? What evidence do I have that it is helping my students?
3 Management	How can I develop the skills to create a more rigorous classroom? How can I do this with everything else I have to do?
2 Personal	How will increasing rigor impact me? What will my plan to improve rigor look like?
1 Informational	How do you increase rigor in your classroom? Where do I get information?
0 Awareness	What is rigor? Things are fine; I'm not concerned about it.

Adapted From: Hord, Rutherford, Huling-Austin & Hall, 1987

Leaders need to recognize the diverse feelings and concerns when you begin to work on improving rigor. Individuals progress through the stages in a developmental manner (see Chapter Ten). Everyone will not move at the same pace or have the same intensity of feeling.

Personal concerns (awareness, informational, personal) often characterize your first steps. As you begin to launch your plans, management concerns emerge. Then, once you are under way teachers become more interested in the effects of rigor on students and on their classrooms.

Check Your Own Commitment

When resistance builds to increasing rigor, it is critical that you are clear about your own commitment. Teachers and families look to you, as the leader, for guidance. It's classic leadership. What you pay attention to becomes important.

The following self-assessment can be used to measure your support for increasing the rigor of your school.

Do These Describe You as a Leader? Use This Scale:

1—Strongly Disagree   4—Agree
2—Disagree   5—Strongly Agree
3—Neutral

I'm open to new ideas and suggestions for improving rigor in my school.	1	2	3	4	5
I'm enthusiastic about increasing rigor.	1	2	3	4	5
I'm an active and enthusiastic learner.	1	2	3	4	5
I participate in professional development with my teachers and staff.	1	2	3	4	5
I am an attentive participant in professional development.	1	2	3	4	5
I talk with teachers about ways to improve rigor in their classrooms.	1	2	3	4	5
I visit classrooms specifically to observe and learn about our work to improve rigor.	1	2	3	4	5
I model the use of good instruction in meetings and other work with teachers.	1	2	3	4	5

Work to Change Attitudes

Principals and teachers often complain that individuals or groups of their colleagues have negative attitudes about students, about the school, or about plans to increase rigor. Too often we take negative attitudes for granted and assume that nothing will change them.

Positive attitudes are critical to the success of your plans to increase rigor. A positive attitude is a prerequisite for real improvements.

Our attitudes come from our life experiences. They are learned. We develop them from dealing with family members, with trying new things, from talking with people who were persuasive or influential. Because of these origins our attitudes are individual and personal, each individual's attitude is unique.

Information is rarely enough to change anyone's attitude. Psychologists have identified three approaches to changing attitudes—cognitive, social, and behavioral.

Approaches to Attitude Change

♦ Cognitive approaches focus on changing the way people think about something like rigor. This is frequently done by sharing information or using persuasive communication.

♦ Behavioral approaches use rewards and punishments. Since most people repeat behaviors that are rewarded and avoid those that are punished, such an approach can ultimately be used to shape beliefs about rigor.

♦ Social approaches rely on our tendency to do things like people we admire. We are more likely to copy their beliefs and behaviors. Providing examples of respected teachers with rigorous classrooms is an example of the approach.

What a Leader Can Do

There are things that a leader can do to change the attitudes and beliefs of those with whom they work. Cognitive dissonance occurs when people become aware of two contradictory beliefs they hold. It is the uncomfortable feeling we get when we recognize that something we believe to be true may not be. As soon as people become aware of the dissonance they must do something about it by reducing the dissonance.

New information often produces cognitive dissonance. It forces us to respond in one of three ways—deny the information, alter our behavior, or alter or rationalize our beliefs.

The following model uses these three approaches to provide an example of a plan for changing attitudes and beliefs about instructional rigor.

Cognitive Approaches	♦ Share data about ways to improve rigor ♦ Provide professional development and other resources about rigor ♦ Share evidence of successful rigorous classrooms
Behavioral Approaches	♦ Provide training and instructional resources for teachers implementing greater rigor ♦ Provide additional released time for teachers to work with colleagues on instructional strategies for improving rigor
Social Approaches	♦ Establish mentor/buddy teams among teachers working on rigor ♦ Showcase practices used by teachers to increase rigor ♦ Provide an opportunity for testimonials about the success of increasing rigor at staff meetings

Focus the Conversation on Students

It seems so obvious to always think about students first. But we've found that when complex and difficult issues arise, student interests are often secondary to the interests of teachers, parents, or community. Part of the problem is that everything that people want to do is always described as being "in the best interests of students." Often diametrically opposed ideas are both described that way.

William Roberts, Principal of Los Altos High School in Hacienda Heights, CA, led significant changes in his school's program. He said that the always asked his staff, "How would you want your child to be treated? What would you want their program to be like?" He found that for many of his teachers those questions forced them to consider the needs of their students through their perspective as a parent. It changed the conversation.

There are some specific ways that you can ensure that improving rigor focuses first on students. As we said earlier, use an inclusive process. Second, ensure that the conversation is guided by a shared vision for improving rigor in your school.

Grading

Some of the greatest resistance usually arises around grading practices, assigning grades for student work. It's one of the most controversial issues related to increasing rigor. A teacher once told Barbara "the only thing my students and their parents care about is an A."

Thomas Guskey and Jane Bailey (2001) described six major purposes of grading:

1. Communicate achievement status
2. Provide information students can use for self-evaluation
3. Select, identify, and group students
4. Provide incentives for students to learn
5. Evaluate the effectiveness of instructional programs
6. Provide evidence of students' lack of effort or responsibility (p. 51)

Each of these purposes is acceptable but, too often, we don't think about grades and their impact on students. We've learned that there is no perfect way to grade. But there are steps you can take to minimize the negative aspects of grading.

Grading is an important topic, especially when you work to increase rigor. It deserves more attention than we can provide here, but in *Rigor is Not a Four-Letter Word* (2008) Barbara identified six ways to minimize the negative aspects of grading.

Minimize Negative Aspects of Grading

- ◆ Recognize the value of grading to students, families, and others
- ◆ Shift the emphasis to learning
- ◆ Provide clear guidelines
- ◆ Require quality work
- ◆ Communicate clearly
- ◆ Be patient

First, recognize that grades are of value to students, families, and others. It may be for college admission or for affirmation of their worth. Regardless, grades are important.

Interpreting Music Data Rubric

Title/Topic **Louisiana's Musical Landscape**   Name _____   Date _____

Task: Complete the *Musical Elements Chart*, the *Music Genres and Venues Worksheet*, and the *Music Prove It*, and present information you learned in mural, poster, oral or written report, timeline, map, skit, or game.

Performance Element	Outstanding 20 pts.	15	Great 10 pts.	5	Not yet 0 pts	Possible	Actual
Discrimination	• Listened attentively; related musical excerpts to regions of the state.		• Listened to musical excerpts, but did not relate all of them to regions of the state.		• Not attentive during listening activity; relied on others to relate music to regions of the state.	20	
Identification	• Identified all musical elements present in excerpts; identified cultural practices that affect music.		• Identified some musical elements in excerpts; cultural practices that affect music not defined for all excerpts.		• Could not identify musical elements or cultural practices.	20	
Interpreting Information	• Categorized musical excerpts using all six musical elements; compared and contrasted recordings; recognized cultural characteristics that determine musical style.		• Categorized musical excerpts using most of the musical elements; most comparisons and contrasts were relevant; recognized some cultural characteristics that determine musical style.		• Information has not been interpreted; jumps to conclusions without carefully categorizing characteristics.	20	
Describing	• Used appropriate vocabulary to describe all genres and musical elements heard in musical excerpts.		• Described most genres and elements; some descriptions not appropriate.		• Used inappropriate descriptions for genres and elements.	20	
Disseminating Information	• Designed and created a mural, poster, oral or written report, timeline, map, skit, or game that effectively interprets the relationship of genres of music to Louisiana regions.		• Designed and created a mural, poster, oral or written report, timeline, map, skit, or game to interpret the relationship of genres of music to Louisiana regions, presentation lacking in clarity.		• Mural, poster, oral or written report, timeline, map, skit, or game not completed.	20	

Bowman, Paddy, Maida Owens, and Sylvia Bienvenu. "Interpreting Music Data." Louisiana Voices Educator's Guide, www.louisianavoices.org, Unit VI: Louisiana's Musical Landscape, Lesson 1 Music Around the State: Sound and Place. 2003.

It is also important to shift the emphasis to learning, not just grades. This is not easy and takes time. Students and their families will probably never ignore grades completely but you can begin by working with teachers to shift the emphasis to student learning.

Providing clear guidelines and a clear rubric for all projects and key assignments is also important. For many students, they don't know what "good" looks like and then teachers become frustrated when quality work is not produced.

Use of a "Not Yet" grading scale for projects and assignments shifts the emphasis to learning and allows students to revise and resubmit work until it is at an acceptable level. Requiring quality work, work that meets your expectations, lets students know you value learning, not just completion of an assignment.

Be sure to communicate your expectations clearly. Students and families need to know school and classroom practices for grades. They need to know about homework and what happens if it is not completed. We often find schools where teachers are asked to provide a written grading policy so that their procedures are clear.

Finally, be patient. For most schools grading is a reality we must live with. It takes time to change practices and for teachers to gain confidence with a new approach to grading. As with students, the "Not Yet" grading policy applies to you and your work to deal with grading and rigor in your school.

Stable or Declining Resources

No issue impacts schools more intensely than the current economic malaise. Virtually every school faces a future impacted by stable or declining resources. At the same time schools are accountable for assuring that every student receives a quality education.

Schools are caught between the expectation that student performance will improve, and the reality that there are fewer human and financial resources to support new program.

These economic realities present a real challenge when you are committed to improving the rigor of your school. Too often, the response is to "stay put" and defer improvements or to look for ways to reduce programs and services.

Almost universally the issue becomes one of how to be both more efficient and more effective. You are expected to sustain your efforts to improve rigor while being even more efficient in the use of your resources.

There are generally three responses to this dilemma. First, you can identify areas where you might reduce expenditures. One district we know considered reducing their classroom supply budget but quickly recognized that even if they eliminated the entire budget it would not solve their budget shortfall.

You can also consider alternative ways of doing some of the things you are already doing. For example, some rural schools find that going to a four-day week reduces the cost of transportation, food service, and office support. Those savings can then be used to support instruction.

The third approach is to prioritize what you are doing. This is very difficult because, even when you use data, the decision almost always is seen as valuing one program more than others. When you prioritize you must anchor your decisions in your school's vision and mission. For example, you would not want to eliminate programs that provide additional support to students if your vision is one where every student is expected to achieve at very high levels.

More Efficient and More Effective

◆ Identify instructional practices that have low cost but high impact on student rigor

◆ Reduce programs that are high cost but yield low student performance or have low impact on student rigor

◆ Make sure every practice supports your vision of a more rigorous school

---

Your vision of a more rigorous school does not need to be set-aside during tough economic times. As we've described, we believe the key to improving rigor is what goes on in each classroom. It is the curricular, instructional, and assessment practices used by your teachers. Momentum in the classroom can be maintained even in difficult times.

However, you may need to reconsider how you provide many of the essential supports needed for more rigorous classrooms. You may want to work with other schools or districts to share professional development resources. You might want to find a local business leader who would support your advocacy efforts with families and the community. Or you might want to increase your efforts to identify volunteers, such as senior citizens, to work with students.

These challenging decisions are almost always better when teachers, families, and other stakeholder groups were included. Use many of the tools we discussed earlier to assure that the decisions support your vision and make the meetings productive.

Turnover in Leadership

Many schools face regular turnover in leadership. A recent study of retirement trends reported that over 50% of principals could retire in the next five years.

Besides the possibility of retirement, the career track for many principals is to move to larger schools with greater responsibility or to a central office or superintendent's position.

Leadership changes present a real challenge for sustaining your commitment to improved rigor. There are several things that you can do to increase leadership capacity in your school and assure a continued commitment to the shared vision.

Expand Your Definition of Leadership

One of the most important things a principal does is expand leadership capacity in others. In some schools this may mean the formal leaders—assistant principal, department chairs, team leaders. But we believe leadership goes beyond these formal roles. You will want to develop the leadership skills of a cross-section of your staff.

Develop Leadership Capacity

There are many ways you can nurture the leadership skills among school staff. It involves creating a school with a variety of leadership roles, opportunity for inquiry and reflection, and the chance to learn and develop new skills.

Some ways to develop leadership capacity include asking someone to work closely with others as part of a committee or leadership team. You might invite a teacher to shadow a school leader for a day and then talk with them about their observations. Or you might challenge them to work with others to solve a "real-life" problem in the school.

> ### *Ways to Help Others Develop Leadership Capacity*
>
> Expand their skills and knowledge base:
>
> - Invite them to work on a project outside their area of expertise;
> - Ask them to help screen and interview potential employees;
> - Encourage them to attend district level meetings with you; and
> - Ask them to work with you in dealing with a challenging parent.
>
> Invite them to work on school improvement projects:
>
> - Ask them to serve on the school leadership team;
> - Ask them to lead a book study group; and
> - Invite them to lead a curriculum planning committee.
>
> Provide opportunities to observe and reflect:
>
> - Encourage them to maintain a journal and reflect on the "good," "bad," or "flawed" leaders they know and observe; and
> - Talk with them about how and why you handled a situation as you did.
>
> Support their participation in professional development:
>
> - Ask them to serve as a mentor of a new teacher;
> - Encourage them to join and be involved with a professional organization; and
> - Ask them to present information to the staff after attending a conference or other professional development activity.

Adapted from: Practical Suggestions for Developing Leadership Capacity (NASSP, 2009)

Commit and Recommit to the Vision

Sustainability is a function of shared vision, a commitment to continuous learning, and to collaborative work.

You will want to maintain your sense of purpose by using the language of your vision for improved rigor when working with teachers, families, and community groups. Keeping the vision "front and center" will help maintain a focus on forward momentum.

As you work to sustain your vision you will want to consider some of the following ideas.

Ways to Sustain The Vision

- Talk about the vision when meeting with teachers, families, and community
- Identify leaders from among your staff who should be provided opportunity to develop their leadership skills
- Guard against low-priority projects that can take attention away from your vision of improved rigor
- Work closely with new staff so that they are familiar with your school's culture and your vision for increased rigor
- Always provide time to reflect and process the work at the end of faculty meetings or other professional development
- Rotate leadership responsibilities in order to expand capacity
- Celebrate your successes

The most successful schools are those where leadership is broad and deep. In these schools many people have formal and informal leadership roles and there is a shared commitment to deepening their collective leadership capacity.

Final Thoughts

Every study of effective schools has found that they are lead by a skillful principal. Principals do have an impact on students in their school and on the teachers who work with their students.

We applaud your decision to embark on the journey to create a more rigorous school. As you continue your work we encourage you to use the seven tools that are part of the COMPASS model. We'd enjoy learning about your successes and your challenges. Please contact us at http://www.rigorineducation.com.

References

Achieve. (2007, April). *Aligned expectations? A closer look at college admissions and placement tests.* Washington, DC: Achieve.

Achieve. (2007, April). *Closing the expectations gap 2007: An annual 50-state progress report on the alignment of high school policies with the demands of college and work.* Washington, DC: Achieve.

ACT. (2006). *Reading between the lines: What the ACT reveals about college readiness in reading.* Iowa City, IA: Author.

ACT. (2007). *Rigor at risk: Reaffirming quality in the high school core curriculum.* Iowa City, IA: Author.

ACT. (2008). *The forgotten middle.* Iowa City, IA: Author.

Adventure Associates (2009). Teamwork Skills: Fist-to-Five Measuring Support. Retrieved online May 30, 2009, from http://www. adventureassoc.com/resources/newsletter/nltc-fist-to-five.html

American Diploma Project. (2004). *Ready or not: Creating a high school diploma that counts.* Washington, DC: Achieve.

Barth, R. (2006). Improving relationships within the schoolhouse. *Educational Leadership, 63*(6), 8–13.

Beane, J. (2001). Rigor and relevance: Can we have our cake and eat it too? Paper presented at the Annual Conference of the National Middle School Association, Washington.

Blackburn, B. (2000). *Barriers and facilitators to effective staff development: Perceptions from award-winning practitioners.* Unpublished doctoral dissertation, University of North Carolina at Greensboro, Greensboro.

Blackburn, B. (2005). *Classroom motivation from A to Z.* Larchmont, NY: Eye on Education.

Blackburn, B. (2007). *Classroom instruction from A to Z.* Larchmont, NY: Eye on Education.

Blackburn, B. (2008a). *Literacy from A to Z.* Larchmont, NY: Eye on Education.

Blackburn, B. (2008b). *Rigor is Not a Four-Letter Word.* Larchmont, NY: Eye on Education.

Blackburn, B., & Williamson, R. (2009). Increasing rigor. *Principal Leadership, 9*(8), 28–31.

Bogess, J. A. (2007). The three Rs redefined for a flat world. *Techniques: Connecting Education & Careers, 82,* 62.

Bolman, L., & Deal, T. (2003). *Reframing organizations: Artistry, choice and leadership* (3rd ed.). San Francisco, CA: Jossey-Bass.

Borko, H. (2004). Professional development and teacher learning: Mapping the terrain. *Educational Researcher, 33*(8), 3–15.

Bower, M. (1996). *Will to manage.* New York: McGraw-Hill.

Cavanagh, S. (2004). Bush plan calls for more rigor in vocational education. *Education Week, 23,* 30.

Collins, J. (2009). *How the mighty fall.* New York: Harper Collins.

Daggett, W. R. (2005). Achieving academic excellence through rigor and relevance. *International Center for Leadership in Education.* Retrieved April 13, 2008, from http://www.leadered.com/pdf/Academic_Excellence.pdf

David, J. (2009). Collaborative inquiry. *Educational Leadership, 66*(4), 87–88.

Davis, S., Darling-Hammond, L., LaPointe, M., & Meyerson, D. (2005). *School leadership study: Developing successful principals.* Stanford, CA: Stanford University, Stanford Educational Leadership Institute.

Deal, T., & Kennedy, A. (1982). *Corporate Cultures: The rites and rituals of corporate life.* Reading, MA: Addison-Wesley.

Deal, T., & Peterson, K. (1990). *The principal's role in shaping school culture.* Washington, DC: U.S. Department of Education.

Deal, T., & Peterson, K. (1999). *Shaping school culture: The heart of leadership.* San Francisco, CA: Jossey-Bass.

DuFour, Ri., DuFour, Re., Eaker, R. & Many, T. (2006). *Learning by doing: A handbook for professional learning communities at work.* Bloomington, IN: Solution Tree.

Dyer, C. (n.d.). *Teaching for rigor and relevance.* (PowerPoint presentation). Bernards Township Public Schools.

Fletcher, A. (2002). Fist-to-five consensus-building. *Freechild Project.* Retrieved July 1, 2009, from http://www.freechild.org/Firestarter/Fist2Five.htm

Fordham Institute (2009). *Growing pains in advanced placement program: Do tough tradeoffs lie ahead?* Washington, DC: Author.

Fullan, M. (2001a). *Leading in a culture of change*. San Francisco: Jossey-Bass.

Fullan, M. (2001b). *The new meaning of educational change* (3rd ed.). New York: Teachers College Press.

Garmston, R., & Wellman, B. (1999). *The adaptive school: A sourcebook for developing collaborative groups*. Norwood, MA: Christopher-Gordon.

Ginsberg, M. B., & Brown, C. (2009). A day's worth of data. *Educational Leadership, 66*(4), 75–79.

Glickman, C., Gordon, S., & Ross-Gordon, J. (2004). *Supervision and instructional leadership: A developmental approach* (6th ed.). Boston, MA: Allyn & Bacon.

Gold, Y., & Roth, R. (1999). *The transformational helping professional: Mentoring and supervising reconsidered*. Boston: Allyn & Bacon.

Guskey, T. R., & Bailey, J. M. (2001). *Developing grading and reporting systems for student learning*. Thousand Oaks, CA: Corwin Press.

Hechinger Institute (2009). *Understanding and reporting on academic rigor*. New York: Teachers' College Press.

Hord, S. (2007). *Professional learning communities: Communities of continuous inquiry and improvement*. Austin, TX: Southwest Educational Development Laboratory.

Hord, S. (2009). Professional learning communities. *Journal of Staff Development, 30*(1), 40–43.

Hord, S., & Sommers, W. (2009). *Leading professional learning communities*. Thousand Oaks, CA: Corwin.

Hord, S., Rutherford, W., Huling-Austin, L., & Hall, G. (1987). *Taking charge of change*. Alexandria, VA: Association for Supervision and Curriculum Development.

Hoy, W., & Tarter, C. J. (2008). *Administrators solving the problems of practice: Decision-making concepts, cases, and consequences* (3rd ed.). Boston: Pearson Education.

Jackson, R. R. (2009). *Never work harder than your students and other principles of great teaching*. Alexandria, VA: Association for Supervision and Curriculum Development.

Johnston, J. H., & Williamson, R. (1998). Listening to four communities. *NASSP Bulletin, 82*(597), 44–52.

Kohm, B., & Nance, B. (2007). *Principals who learn: Asking the right questions, seeking the best solutions*. Alexandria, VA: Association for Supervision and Curriculum Development.

Leithwood, K., Louis, K., Anderson, S., & Wahlstrom, K. (2004). How leadership influences student learning. Report commissioned by the Wallace Foundation. Retrieved April 19, 2009, from www.allacefoundation.org/KnowledgeCenter/KnowledgeTopics/EducationLeadership/HowLeadershipInfluencesStudent Learning.htm

Marx, G. (2006). *Sixteen trends, their profound impact on our future: Implications for students, education, communities, and the whole of society*. Alexandria, VA: Educational Research Service.

Marzano, R., Pickering, D., & Pollock, J. (2001). *Classroom instruction that works: Research-based strategies for increasing student achievement.* Alexandria, VA: Association for Supervision and Curriculum Development.

Maslow, A. H. (1968). *Toward a psychology of being.* New York: John Riley.

National Assessment of Educational Progress. (2007). Mapping state proficiency standards. Retrieved November 5, 2009, from http://nces.ed.gov/nationsreportcard/pubs/studies/2010456.asp

National Association of Secondary School Principals. (2009). Practical suggestions for developing leadership capacity in others. Retrieved November 2, 2009, from www.principals.org/s_nassp/sec.asp?CID=1600&DID=56566

National Commission on Excellence in Education. (1983). *A nation at risk: The imperative for educational reform.* Washington, DC: Institute for educational Leadership.

National High School Alliance. (2006a). *Increasing academic rigor in high schools: Stakeholder perspectives.* Washington, DC: Institute for Educational Leadership.

National High School Alliance. (2006b). *Defining rigor in high school.* Washington, DC: Institute for Educational Leadership.

National Staff Development Council. (2001). *National Staff Development Council's Standards for Staff Development.* Retrieved April 19, 2009, from www.nsdc.org/standards/index.cfm

Peterson, K., & Deal, T. (2002). *The shaping school culture fieldbook.* San Francisco: Jossey-Bass.

Reeves, D. (2003). *Making standards work: How to implement standards-based assessments in the classroom, school, and district.* Englewood, CO: Advanced Learning Press.

Schlechty, P. (1997). *Inventing better schools.* San Francisco: Jossey-Bass.

Schein, E. (1985). *Organizational culture and leadership.* San Francisco, CA: Jossey-Bass.

Schein, E. (2004). *Organizational Culture and leadership* (3rd ed.). San Francisco, CA: Jossey-Bass.

Secretary's Commission on Achieving Necessary Skills. (1992). SCANS Report. Retrieved November 5, 2009, from http://wdr.doleta.gov/SCANS/

Shapiro, J., & Stefkovich, J. (2005). *Ethical leadership and decision-making in education* (2nd ed.). Mahwah, NJ: Lawrence Erlbaum Associates.

Southern Regional Education Board (SREB). (2004). *Using rigor, relevance and relationships to improve student achievement: How some schools do it* (2004 Outstanding Practices). Atlanta, GA: Author.

Strong, R. W., Silver, H.F., & Perrini, M.J. (2001). *Teaching what matters most: Standards and strategies for raising student achievement.* Alexandria, VA: Association for Supervision and Curriculum Development.

Vatterott, C. (2009). *Rethinking homework: Best practices that support diverse needs.* Alexandria, VA: Association for Supervision and Curriculum Development.

Wagner, T. (2008a). *The global achievement gap: Why even our best schools don't each the new survival skills our children need—and what we can do about it.* New York: Basic Books.

Wagner, T. (2008b). Rigor Redefined. *Educational Leadership, 66*(2), 20–24.

Washor, E., & Mojkowski, C. (2006/2007). What do you mean by rigor? *Educational Leadership, 64,* 84–87.

Wasley, P.A., Hampel, R. L., & Clark, R.W. (1997). *Kids and school reform.* San Francisco: Jossey-Bass.

Wasserstein, P. (1995). What middle schoolers say about their schoolwork. *Educational Leadership, 53*(1), 41–43.

Williamson, G. L. (2006). *Student readiness for postsecondary endeavor.* Paper presented at the annual meeting of the American Educational Research Association, San Francisco, CA.

Williamson, R. (2009). *Scheduling to improve student learning.* Westerville, OH: National Middle School Association.

Williamson, R. & Blackburn, B. (2009). *The Principalship from A to Z.* Larchmont, NY: Eye on Education.

Williamson, R., & Johnston, J. H. (1999). Challenging orthodoxy: An emerging agenda for middle level reform. *Middle School Journal, 30*(4), 10–17.

Yeung, B. (2009). Struggling helps students master math. *Edutopia.* Retrieved online at http://www.edutopia.org/math-underachieving-mathnext-rutgers-newark

Printed in the USA/Agawam, MA
October 8, 2014

598740.002